P9-DBI-500

Science at the Edge

Rebuilding the Body

Organ Transplantation

Ann Fullick

Heinemann Library
Chicago, Illinois

Published by Heinemann Library,
an imprint of Reed Educational & Professional Publishing,
Chicago, Illinois

Customer Service 888-454-2279

Visit our website at www.heinemannlibrary.com

Designed by Tinstar Design
Illustrations by Art Construction
Originated by Ambassador Litho Ltd.
Printed and bound in Hong Kong/China

06 05 04 03 02
10 9 8 7 6 5 4 3 2 1

Library of Congress Cataloging-in-Publication Data
Fullick, Ann, 1956-
Rebuilding the body : organ transplantation / Ann Fullick.
p. cm. -- (Science at the edge)
Includes bibliographical references and index.
ISBN 1-58810-700-0
1. Transplantation of organs, tissues, etc.--Juvenile literature. [1. Transplantation of organs, tissues, etc.] I. Title. II. Series.
RD120.76 .F85 2002
617.9'5--dc21
2001006082

Acknowledgments
The publishers would like to thank the following for permission to reproduce photographs: p. 4 Pierre Gleizes/Still Pictures; pp. 5, 8, 10, 12, 22, 29, 32, 55 Science Photo Library; pp. 11, 52 Wellcome Medical Trust; pp. 15, 19T, 41 Popperfoto; p. 15 Sheila Terry/Science Photo Library; pp. 19B, 26, 3 Corbis; p. 21 Mike Schroder/Still Pictures; pp. 23, 27, 33 Medical Photography Portsmouth Hospitals NHS Trust; pp. 27, 43, 47 Amanda Sheehan; p. 34 Joseph Sohm/Corbis; p. 37 Chris Priest/Science Photo Library; p. 39 Frank Spooner Pictures; p. 45 WENN/TV-AM; p. 49 inset Mary Ann McDonald/Corbis; pp. 49, 57 Topham Picturepoint; p. 50 Environmental Images; p. 53 Richard T. Nowitz/Corbis.

Cover photograph reproduced with permission of Still Pictures.

Thanks for their invaluable input to Lucy and Amanda Sheehan and the Sheehan family, Anne Walters, and other members of the Wessex Renal Transplant team at Portsmouth.

Some words are shown in bold, **like this.** You can find out what they mean by looking in the glossary.

Contents

The Organs of the Body

The human body is a masterpiece of biology. It enables us to move around to get food, escape danger, get to school on time, or play football, baseball, or soccer. More than that, the human body takes the food that we eat and turns it into energy we use every day. The body can also get rid of poisons that may be taken in or produced by the body itself. It can survive in a wide range of conditions, use tools, and even help you write a book. All these things are possible because of the complex biology going on inside the human body.

All of the activities of the body are made possible by organs (collections of cells and **tissues** that carry out a major function in the body) working together. Each organ carries out a very specific job within the body. The major organs include the heart, which pumps the blood around the body; the **kidneys,** which balance the water levels in the body and get rid of waste; the eyes, which enable us to see; and the liver, which cleans and purifies the blood. These organs work together to maintain the right conditions inside of your body, regardless of what you are doing or where you are.

The average human being contains billions of cells, miles of tubing, yards of skin, gallons of fluid, and pounds of muscle. Somehow all of this has to be organized to work and to work properly, whatever the demands that are put on the body.

What if things go wrong?

Almost everyone takes his or her body completely for granted until something goes wrong. If anything does go wrong with any of a person's major organs, he or she will be in a very serious situation. The failure of a major organ can cause death. However, in the last 50 years, there has been an enormous increase in the number of people who survive the total failure of one of their body organs, thanks to the development of transplant surgery and organ transplantation. This involves giving a very sick person the healthy organs he or she needs from someone else, often someone who has died very suddenly. There are many thousands of people around the world who are alive today only because they have someone else's heart, kidney, liver, lungs, or small intestine working inside their own bodies, carrying out the important job that their own organs were no longer able to do.

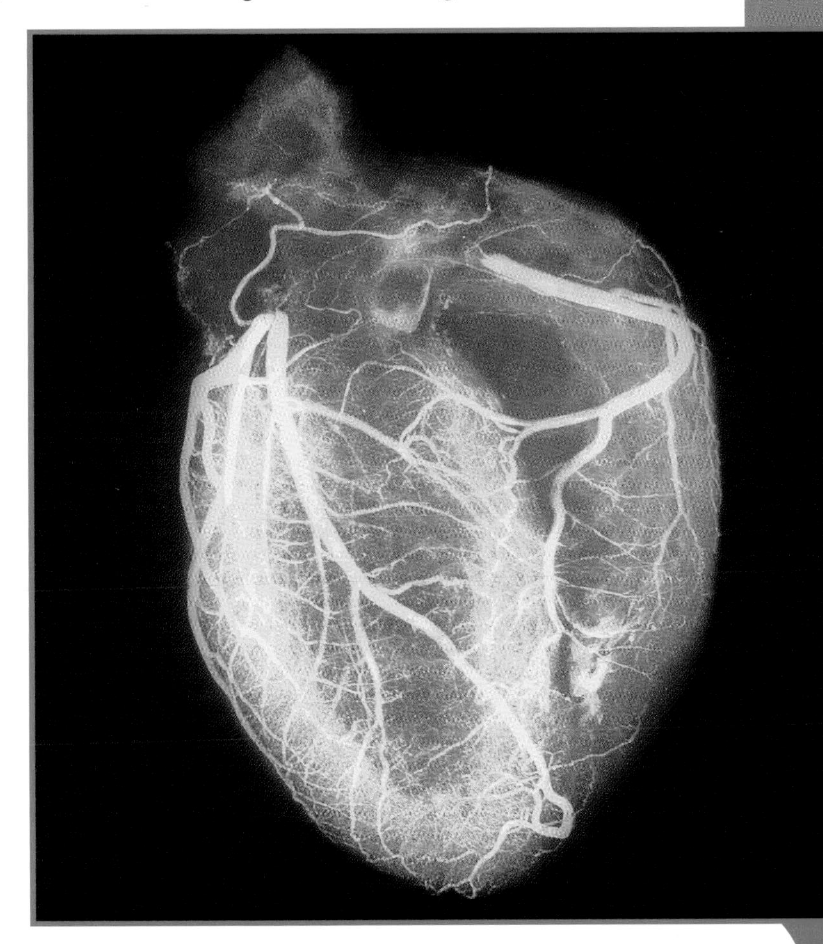

The idea that a complex organ like the heart could be removed and replaced with another one would have seemed completely unbelievable 100 years ago. Yet now, someone somewhere in the world receives a transplanted organ every 27 minutes.

How does the organization work?

The basic unit of a human being is the single cell, which is a jellylike blob contained in a **membrane.** A cell carries out lots and lots of chemical reactions at the same time. In large organisms, such as human beings, cells are often very specialized. This means they carry out one particular job. The structure of these specialized cells is different from the basic cell structure in order to suit the very specialized jobs that they do.

The specialized cells are often grouped together to form a **tissue.** In human beings, connective tissue joins parts of the body together, while nervous tissue carries information around the body, and muscles move the body around.

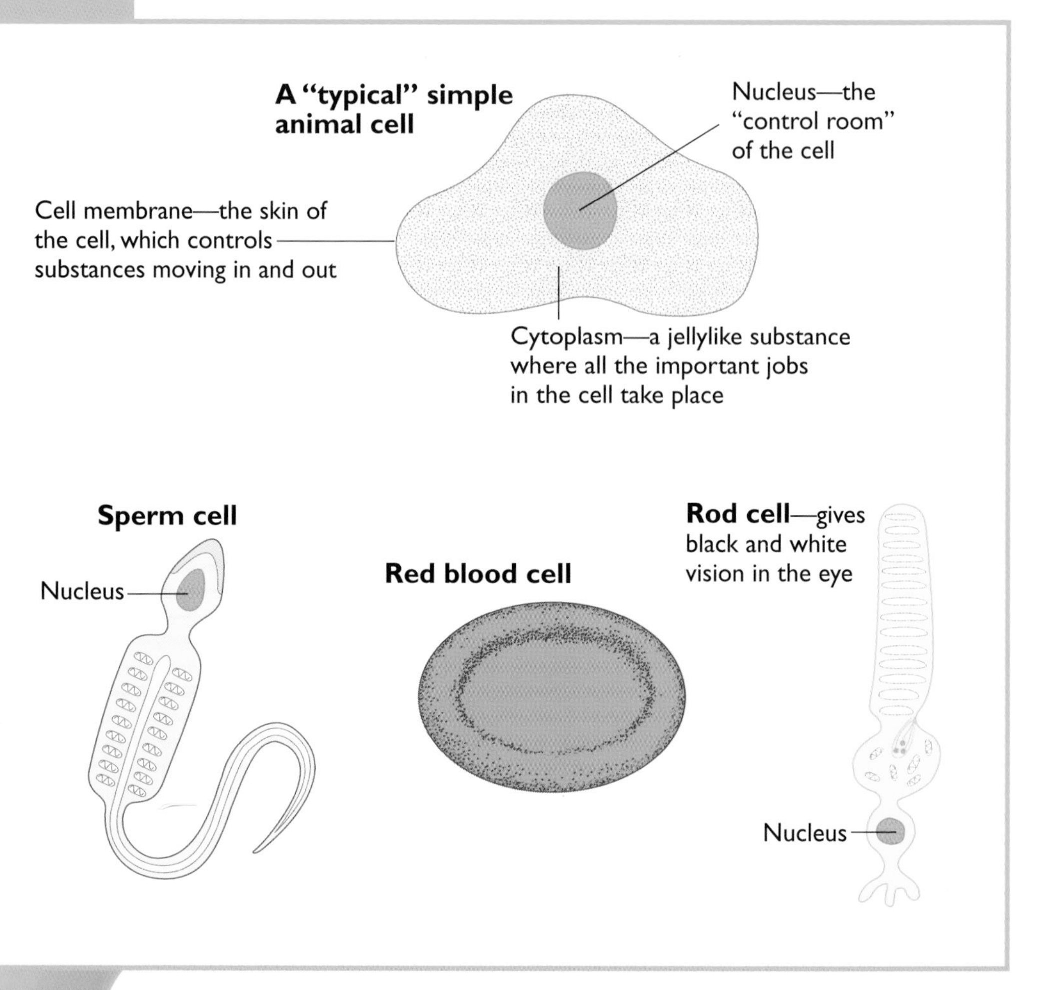

Sometimes cells become so specialized that they have only one function within the body. Good examples of this include sperm, red blood cells, and rod cells, the specialized cells involved in color vision in the human eye.

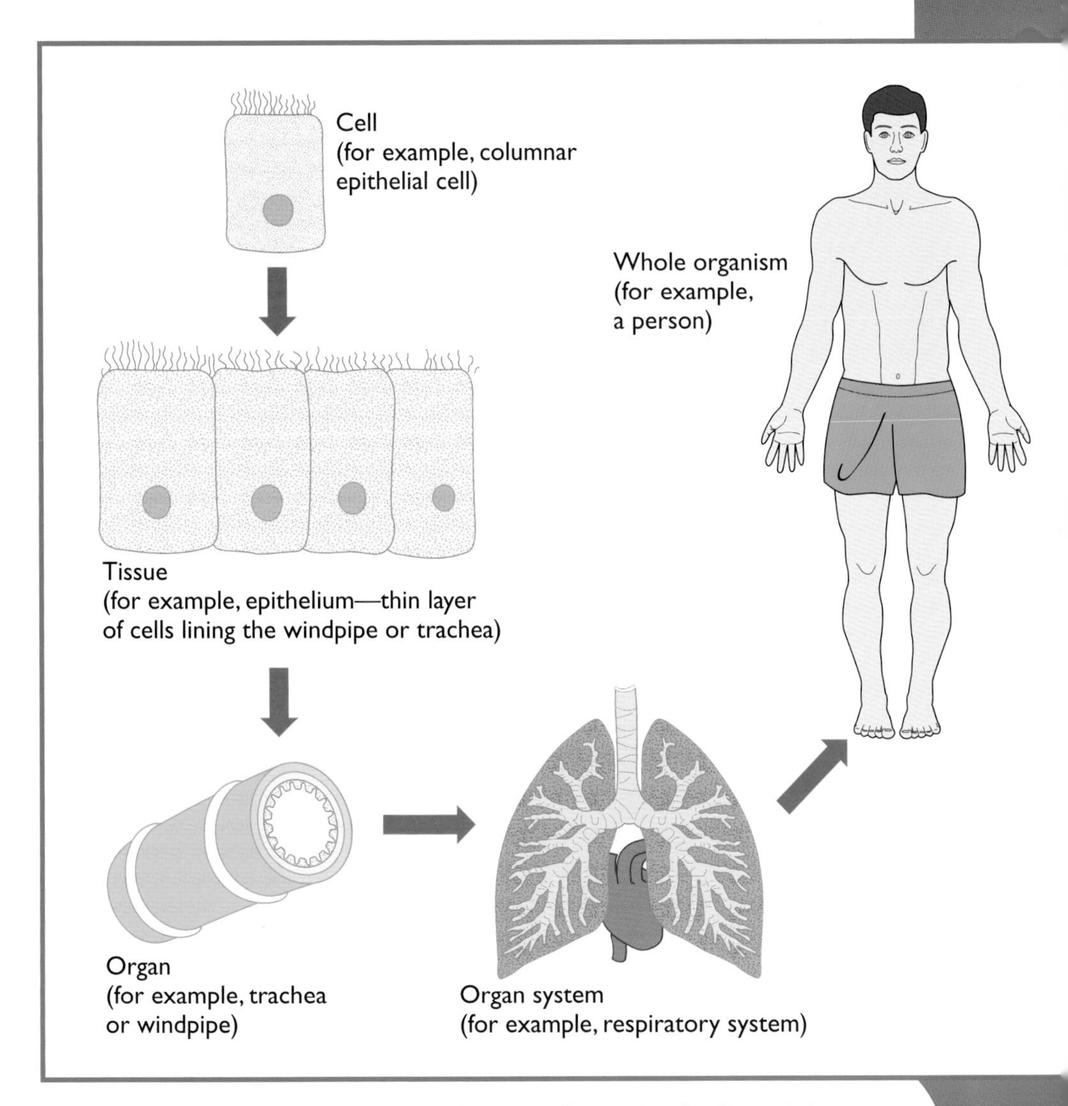

Human organs are made up of groups of specialized cells, and the organ systems are designed to carry out very specific jobs, including getting oxygen into the blood, pumping blood around the body, or hearing what is going on in the environment.

In many living organisms, including human beings, there is another level of organization. Several different tissues work together to form an organ such as the heart, the **kidneys,** or the liver. Each of these organs has its own job. In turn, different organs are combined in **organ systems** to carry out major functions in the body, such as transporting the blood or reproduction.

Understanding the human organs and organ systems makes it clear why it is very serious if they stop working properly.

The heart and lungs

The best known human organs are the heart and the lungs. They are both vital for life. They work together as a team, along with miles of blood vessels, to make up what is called the cardiovascular system. The heart is one of the earliest organs to be formed in the developing human **embryo.**

The heart is basically a bag of muscle that starts to beat about six weeks after an embryo begins developing in the **uterus.** It fills and empties, forcing blood out of the heart to where blood is needed. The right side of the heart sends blood to the lungs to pick up oxygen. The blood also gets rid of the poisonous **carbon dioxide** that has built up as a waste product in the working cells of the body. The left side of the heart sends oxygen-rich blood, which has been through the lungs, around to the rest of the whole body. This supplies all the cells with the oxygen they need for life.

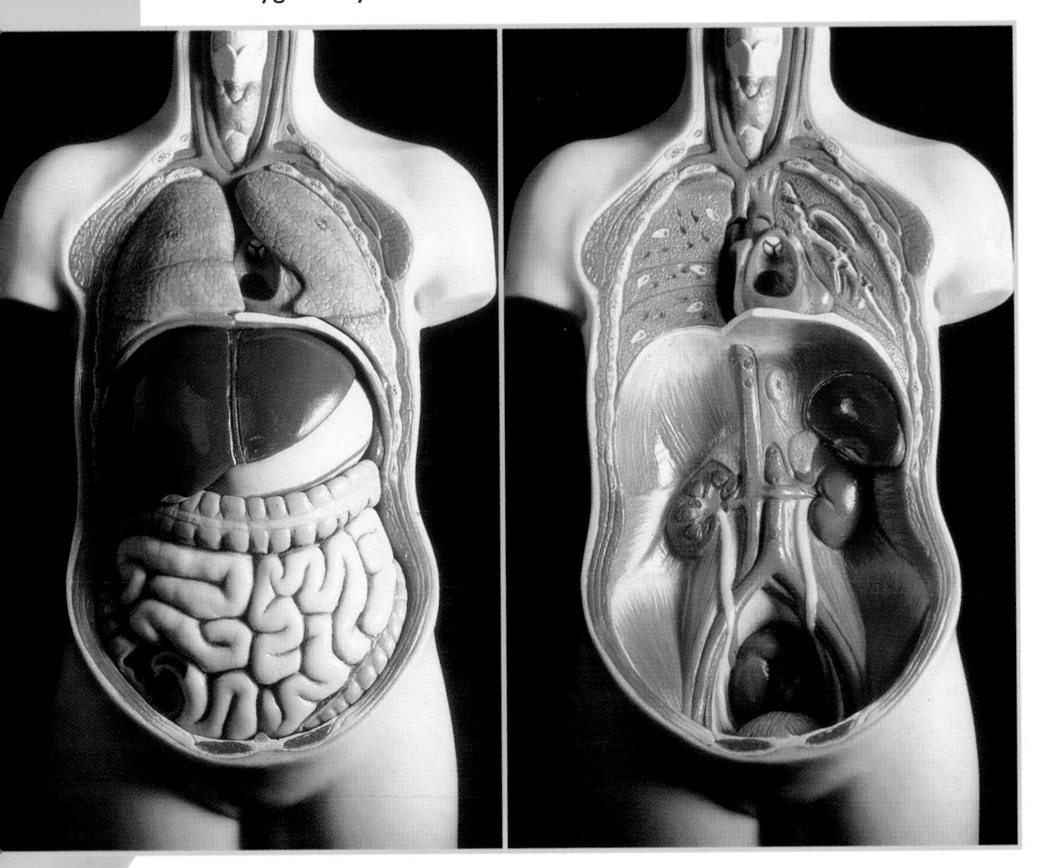

Inside all of us, there are lots of different organs, all doing important jobs that help to keep us alive.

The heart is made up of muscle **tissue** that has its own rich blood supply. It also contains special tissue that makes up the valves of the heart (flaps that stop blood from flowing in the wrong direction) and big blood vessels that allow blood to flow into and out of the heart.

The lungs take the blood from the body and pass it through specially adapted tiny **air sacs.** These allow as much oxygen as possible to be picked up by the blood and allow as much carbon dioxide as possible to be removed from the blood. The process is known as gaseous exchange, and it must take place efficiently if someone is to lead a healthy, active life.

A pair of kidneys

The **kidneys** remove **urea** from the system. Urea is a poisonous waste product that results from the breakdown of **protein** in the diet. The kidneys also remove excess salt and control the water balance of the body. This is very important because if the water balance is not normal, all the cells in the body are in danger of either swelling or shriveling up. Either way, the cells would not work properly, and illness or death could result.

What does a liver do?

Most people know that they have a liver, but they are often unsure about where it is and what it does. The liver is one of the most important organs in the body. It performs about 500 different jobs. It is involved in the control and management of the **carbohydrates,** proteins, and fats we eat. It helps to remove and break down **cholesterol** and other fats and convert them into storage **molecules.** The liver breaks down excess proteins into urea, which can be excreted, and useful amino acids (the chemical building blocks of proteins). It stores a number of substances, makes bile (a liquid that helps in digestion), helps control the body temperature, and breaks down some of the **toxins** taken into the body. Substances such as alcohol and painkillers are toxins. In fact, the liver acts like a personal detoxification (poison-removal) factory by getting rid of harmful chemicals. Obviously, a liver is a very useful organ. When the liver fails, the body is affected in many ways, several of which could lead to death.

Organ Failure!

Most people are born with a set of perfectly healthy organs which then go on to work throughout their lives. After 70, 80, 90, or even 100 years, their hearts, **kidneys,** lungs, and livers may all still be carrying out the tasks they did so many years earlier. However, not everyone is so lucky. **Organ systems** can be damaged in a number of ways or may stop functioning altogether. The effect this has on a person can range from distressing, when, for example, sight or hearing is lost because of damage to the eyes or ears, to completely life-threatening, when organs such as the heart, liver, or kidneys fail.

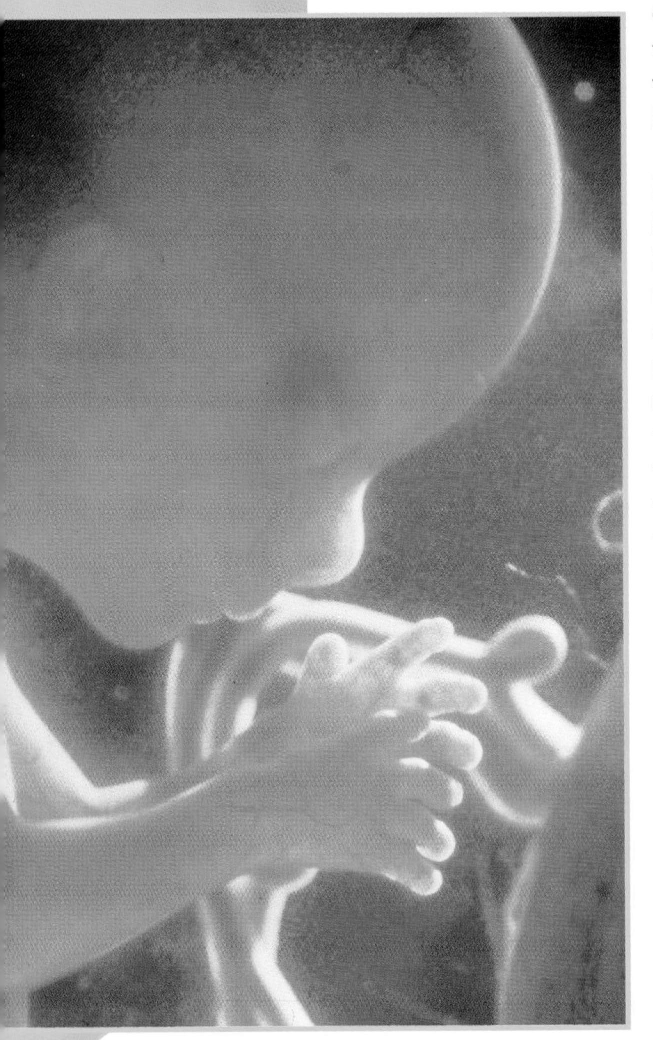

Problems can start even before a person is born. Sometimes organs do not form properly as the **embryo** develops. If the problem shows up on an ultrasound **scan** (a technique using very high frequency sound to see inside the body), then doctors and the parents can prepare. If surgery is possible, it is done shortly after the birth. Sometimes it can even take place while the baby is still developing in the **uterus.** Babies born after this type of surgery heal so well, they are born without a scar. But even with all the technology available today, some babies are still born with unexpected organ problems. When this happens, the worst case is

While a baby is developing in the uterus, many of its main body functions are dealt with by the mother's body through the **placenta.** If the baby's heart or lungs do not work properly, the baby is not greatly affected. But after birth, the baby can be in a serious condition. Some babies die because their organs have failed to develop in the uterus.

that the baby will die before surgery can correct the problem. However, in many cases, the child can be kept alive for at least a few weeks or months. By that time a solution, such as corrective surgery or a transplant, may be found.

Kidney infections

Sometimes people are born with a set of perfectly healthy organs, but develop an **infection** at some stage of their life that attacks and damages an organ beyond repair. For example, if an infection in the urethra (the tube that carries urine from the bladder out of the body) is neglected, the infection can spread up into the bladder and on into the kidneys, causing kidney damage and even kidney failure. However, kidney infections are quite common and are easily and effectively treated with antibiotics. Only multiple, repeated infections over a period of years could result in kidney failure. Without the kidneys, **urea** quickly builds up to **toxic** levels and the water balance of the body is lost. Death will occur a few days after the kidneys fail.

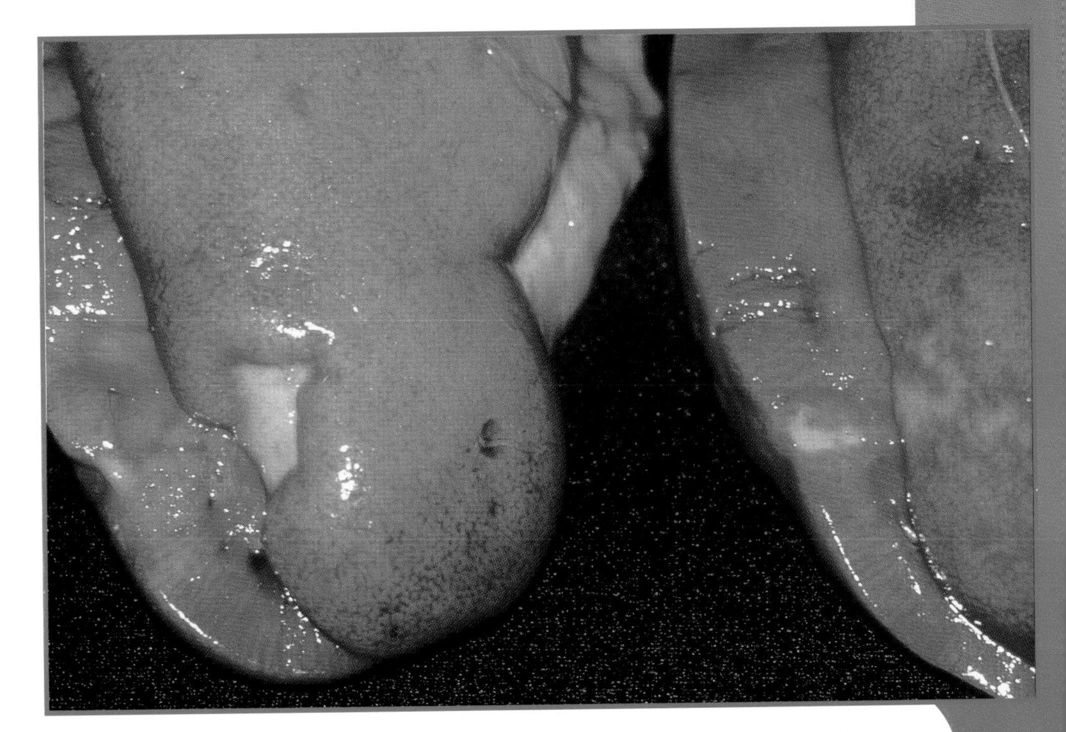

When an infection takes hold, it can destroy an organ with terrifying speed. Within days, healthy kidney **tissue** can be damaged forever. These kidneys suffered damage as a result of a heart disease.

Other infections

The **kidneys** are not the only organs that can be affected by the invasion of **microorganisms. Infections** of the heart can damage the heart muscle so severely that it can no longer pump the blood effectively. A badly damaged heart can cause death even more rapidly than failing kidneys. Hepatitis, a disease that is becoming increasingly common in the developed world, causes massive destruction of liver cells. The same thing happens if the liver is attacked by liver **cancer.**

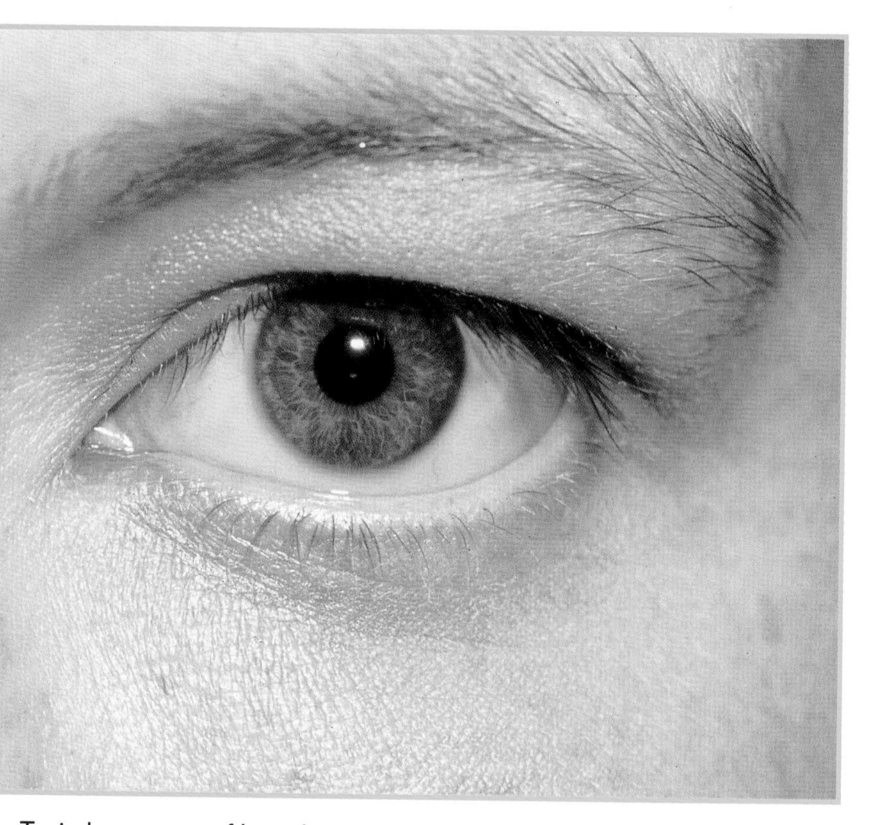

Typical symptoms of liver disease include yellow skin and yellow "whites" of the eyes. Bile, produced from the breakdown of the red blood cells, is not removed by the liver and builds up in the blood, coloring the skin and other **tissues.** This is known as jaundice. The level of jaundice can give an immediate indication of how well the liver is working. In contrast to the skin, feces lacks the color of the bile pigments, and so it appears very pale.

The intestines also can be attacked by infections that damage their lining and affect their ability to absorb food. In the most severe infections, there is multiple organ failure. Even transplant surgery cannot help in these cases.

Gradual damage

Organ failure that results from severe infection does not always happen rapidly. Sometimes the destruction happens relatively slowly. The organ gets weaker over a number of years. This can be caused by progressive illnesses or from damage caused by drugs. Drinking too much alcohol over a period of time can cause permanent liver and brain damage. Smoking cigarettes damages the lungs and the structure of the delicate **air sacs,** which makes it harder and harder to get enough oxygen into the blood. Smoking also affects the heart, making **heart attacks** more likely. If unsuitable drugs are given to a patient, kidney and liver damage can result. High blood pressure is another common cause of damage to organs such as the kidneys. Once the filtering mechanism is damaged, the organs never work properly again.

My kidneys started to fail when I was given a drug to treat another problem. For the first nine and a half years, I coped by managing my diet very carefully—I could only eat small amounts of ***protein*** *and the levels of liquid and salt I took in mattered, too. But eventually I became more and more tired and began to feel really unwell.*

Bernard Everard, a kidney patient, describing the gradual failing of his kidneys when he was in his fifties, after a prescribed drug for another illness caused irreversible kidney damage

Another common cause of organ damage occurs when the coronary arteries, the blood vessels that supply blood to the heart, become narrowed due to a buildup of fatty deposits on the walls. If a clot then forms in the blood and blocks the blood vessel, the muscle walls of the heart are starved of oxygen and may die. This is what is commonly known as a heart attack, or coronary thrombosis. If the heart is severely damaged, it may never work as effectively again, even if the patient survives the attack.

The organs of the body can fail for a number of reasons. Problems can arise at any time from **conception** onward, although the risk of organ failure gets higher with age. However, many babies and young children also face the prospect of a shortened life if some of their vital organs begin to fail. The challenge is to find ways to repair or replace those failing organs and give the patients back their quality of life.

One day Christopher was playing happily with the other children—and a few days later, his life was hanging in the balance and his kidneys had failed completely. The infection struck so quickly, we were all completely stunned.

Ann Fullick, describing the speed at which a neighbor's child was affected by a kidney infection

New Parts for Old

For centuries, doctors have struggled to deal with the life-threatening situation of organ failure, and for most of that time there has been little or nothing they could do. Today, however, there are a number of ways of helping such patients not only to survive but also to live very healthy, active lives. One of the ways to restore a high quality of life to a patient with failing organs is to give them an organ transplant.

The history of organ transplantation goes back a very long way. People recognized that if they could replace damaged or broken body parts, many people could be healed. Progress was very slow, however, because extremely sophisticated science needed to be developed before successful transplants could become possible.

Genuine transplants, in which a new organ is placed in the body of the **recipient** and restores them to a healthy way of life, have taken years to develop.

The compatibility question

Before transplants could help people overcome the problems of failing organs, scientists needed a better understanding of the human body. An important step was developing their knowledge of the human **immune system.** The basis of this system is the ability of cells to know the difference between the cells of the person's body and all other cells. The immune system therefore rejects and destroys transplanted organs because it recognizes them as different. This means that not only have scientists and doctors needed to develop surgical techniques for successful transplants, but they have also had to find ways (for example, by using special drugs) of preventing **rejection** of the new organ. Throughout the first 50 years of the last century, doctors and scientists were gaining knowledge and understanding of how the organs of the body worked. They were also learning to recognize some of the signals used by the immune system. Sir Peter Medawar, often called the father of modern

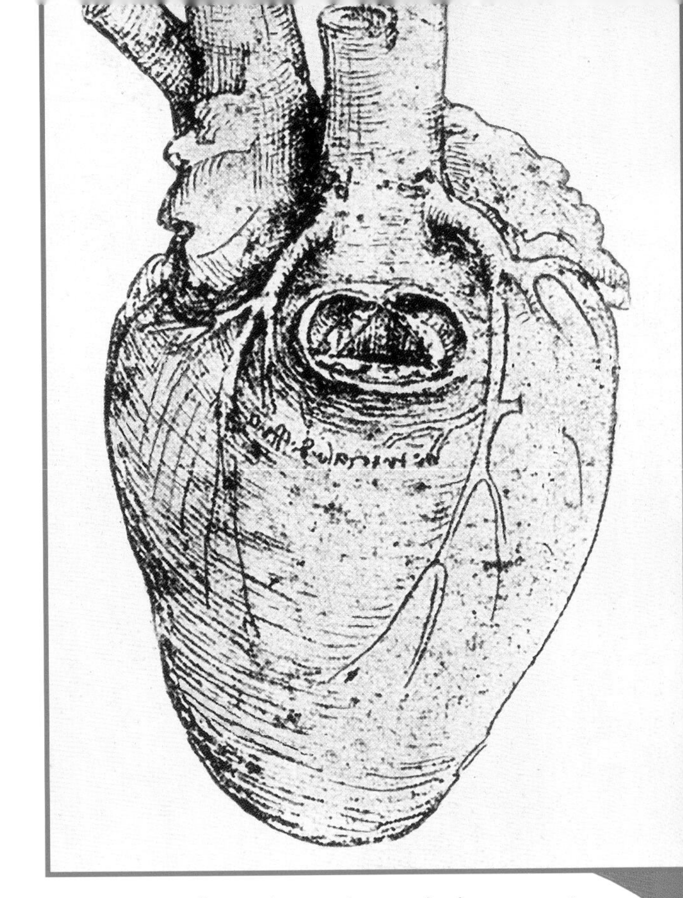

Even in very early times, people tried to understand what was going on inside their bodies. However, their knowledge was limited to what they could find out from examining dead bodies. Over the centuries, many careful drawings of human organs were made, and understanding of the way organs worked grew, too. This drawing of a heart by Leonardo da Vinci dates from the fifteenth century.

immunology (the study of the immune system), did a great deal of pioneering work with **skin grafts** during World War II, leading to a far deeper understanding of the problems of rejection (for more on the immune system and the problems of rejection, see pages 28–29). Scientists and doctors were working toward being able to transplant organs from one person to another, but every phase was an enormous step into the unknown. The patients were very sick and sometimes even dying. Yet if the organ transplant failed to save the patients, the long odds against success would be ignored and the technique would be seen as a failure.

Transplanting kidneys

Kidneys were the first organs to be transplanted successfully. During the early 1950s, a number of experimental kidney transplants were carried out in the United States and France, but they were largely unsuccessful. In 1954, the first successful kidney transplant was carried out by Dr. Joseph E. Murray in Boston, Massachusetts. The **donor** was the living identical twin of the patient, which meant that there were no problems with **rejection.** The cells of identical twins are identical. The **immune system** of the twin who received the donor kidney did not recognize the new kidney as being different. The transplanted kidney worked for another eight years.

Dr. Joseph E. Murray won the Nobel Prize for Medicine in 1990 for his pioneering work on kidney transplantation. He began his surgical career in the United States, working on soldiers burned during World War II, and developed an interest in the problems of avoiding transplant rejection. His work on kidney transplantation helped make a healthy life after transplantation a reality for many thousands of people.

Then in 1959, Murray, working with his colleague Dr. John P. Merrill, performed a kidney allograft (a **graft** from one person to another who is not genetically identical). In this case, the donor and the **recipient** were also twins, but they were not identical. Another team, led by Jean Hamburger in Paris, France, had similar success with another pair of twins. But another big hurdle still had to be overcome. Far more people needed new kidneys than there were donors, and not many people have a convenient twin. Could they use the kidneys from dead donors instead of live donors?

The pioneers—making transplants a reality

In 1962, the team in Boston triumphed again. They transplanted a kidney from a dead donor into a live patient who was given drugs to try to prevent rejection. The new kidney worked successfully for 21 months before it was rejected by the body of the patient. After this, developments came quickly. People were trying all sorts of methods to overcome the problems of rejection. Early methods included irradiating patients (exposing them to electromagnetic radiation) before transplant surgery to destroy their **bone marrow.** This was done to stop the production of **lymphocytes** (white blood cells) because these would attack the new organ. The problem with the irradiation method was that patients sometimes died as a result of it. Special antirejection drugs were also introduced. In the early days, these were very **toxic** and again, the antirejection treatment sometimes killed the patient.

In spite of the early difficulties, a floodgate had opened and new and different organ transplants were taking place every year. In 1963, Dr. Thomas Starzl performed the first human liver transplant at the University of Colorado. However, the patient rejected the transplant and died shortly after the operation. That same year, Dr. James Hardy carried out the first lung transplant in Mississippi. By 1966, the first successful transplant of a pancreas (an organ that makes hormones and digestive enzymes) from a dead donor had taken place. In 1967, Starzl's team performed the first successful liver transplants. Four of their seven patients survived for weeks and even months.

Building on success

Heart transplants became a reality in 1967, with the work of Dr. Christiaan Barnard. After this massive step forward, there was a period during which transplant surgeons and scientists working on **rejection** coordinated their work efforts. Much research was done on improving operating techniques. Antirejection treatment also got better and patient survival times grew longer and longer.

In the 1980s, things moved forward dramatically again. The first combined heart-and-lung transplant took place in 1981. It was carried out by Dr. Norman Shumway and Dr. Bruce Reitz at Stanford University in California. In 1988, Dr. David Grant, operating in Ontario, Canada, achieved the first successful transplant of a small intestine. Since then, through the 1990s and into the twenty-first century, great improvements have been made in antirejection drugs. The chances of a transplant being rejected by the body of the **recipient** have been much reduced, and transplant surgery has become increasingly successful.

There has also been an increase in the number of organs that can be transplanted at one time. Multiple-organ transplants, with up to four different **donor** organs being given to a single patient, have become a reality, although they are still relatively rare. The most common organs to be transplanted in this way are the liver and various other **abdominal organs,** such as the small and large intestines.

The big one—transplanting hearts

The beating of the heart is so closely associated with life that it is almost impossible to imagine that someone could have their heart removed and survive the experience. Yet this is what happened in 1967, when Dr. Christiaan Barnard in Cape Town, South Africa, carried out the first-ever successful human heart transplant. The patient, a middle-aged man named Louis Washkansky, was given the heart of a young 23-year-old woman who had died in a car accident. The whole world was amazed at what had been achieved. Louis lived for eighteen days with his new heart beating in his chest before dying of a lung **infection.** A second attempt, by an American team in New York, failed when the patient died after only six hours. However, in 1968, Phillip Blaiberg received a new heart in the second transplant carried out by Dr. Barnard, and he lived to enjoy a relatively normal life for nearly two years. These days, heart transplant surgery hardly even makes local headlines.

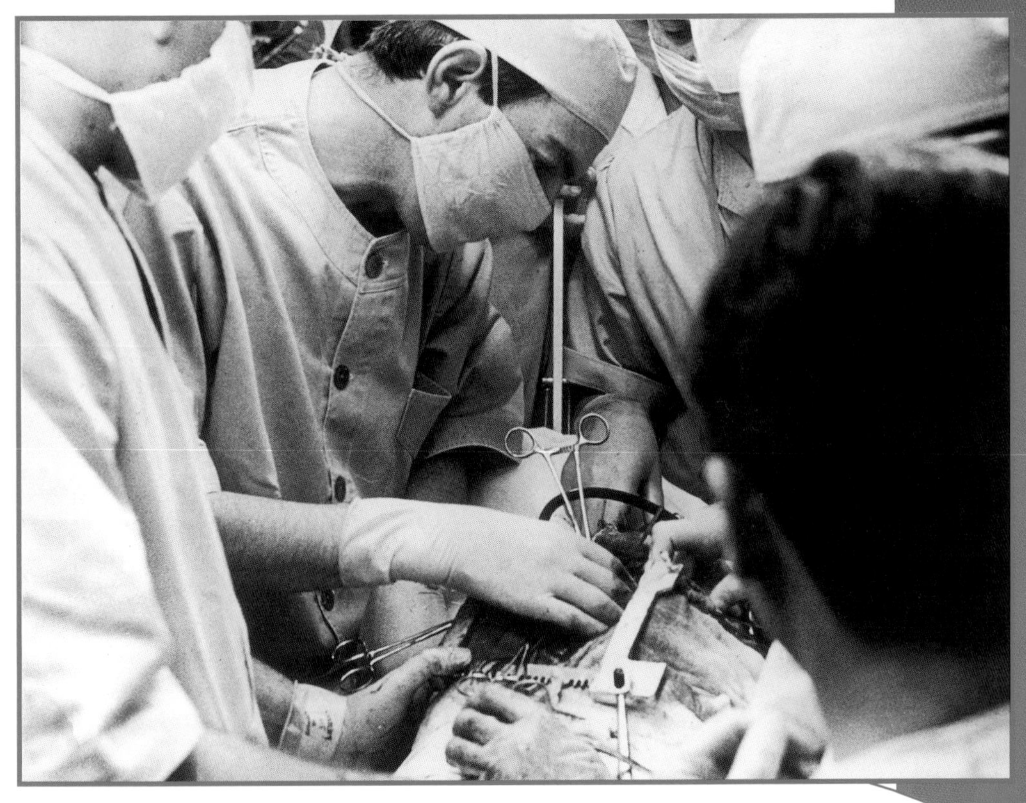

The pioneering work of people like Dr. Joseph E. Murray, Dr. Thomas Starzl, and Dr. Christiaan Barnard paved the way for organ transplants to become a recognized way of treating patients with total organ failure. Dr. Barnard is shown above carrying out an experimental operation on a dog. However, it is important to remember patients such as Louis Washkansky (shown below) and Phillip Blaiberg and their families. Without their bravery and the enormous generosity of the families who donated organs, none of this progress would have been possible.

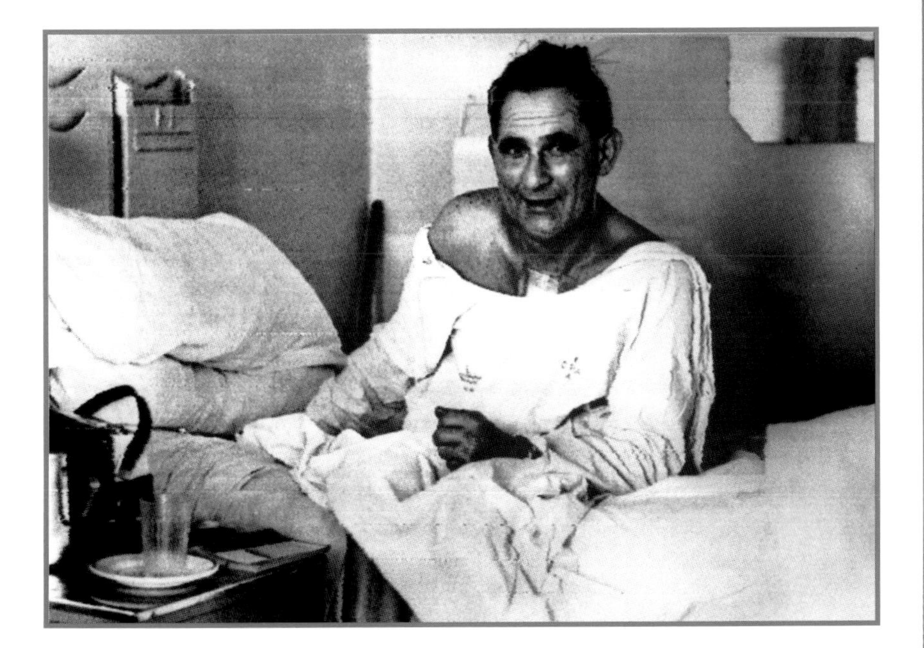

How Is It Done?

If a battery runs out in a toy, it is easily replaced. When a lightbulb stops working, it takes just a few moments to remove the old bulb and put in a new one. When organs of the body fail for whatever reason, replacing them is not nearly so simple.

When a potential **donor** organ becomes available, there is a great deal to do. The **tissue** type of the donor must be matched as closely as possible with a person needing an organ transplant. There are two operating teams working at the same time, sometimes in the same hospital, sometimes in other parts of the country or even in another country. One team removes the organs from the body of the organ donor and packs them in specially prepared boxes for transporting to the operating room, where they are needed for a transplant. Meanwhile, the other team prepares the **recipient** to receive a new organ.

It is important that the donor organ is ready and waiting in the operating room before the recipient's diseased organ is removed. The organ may have to be transported hundreds of miles, and a quick delivery is very important.

Keeping organs fresh

It is vitally important that the donor organs are kept healthy and functional once they have been removed from the donor's body. This is done by washing the blood out of the organs using chilled preservation fluid, which produces a state of "suspended animation" in the organ. This means the vital functions of the organs temporarily stop, but they will return when the organs are connected to a body system again. They are stored in this fluid, surrounded by ice, to keep them at 39.2°F (4°C) while they are transported to wherever they are needed. If ice actually came into contact with the tissue, it would freeze it and cause permanent damage, and the organ would be of no use.

The preservation fluids are very specialized. Research goes on all the time to improve them so that the organs can survive out of the body for longer periods of time. The fluids may cost as much as $215 per quart.

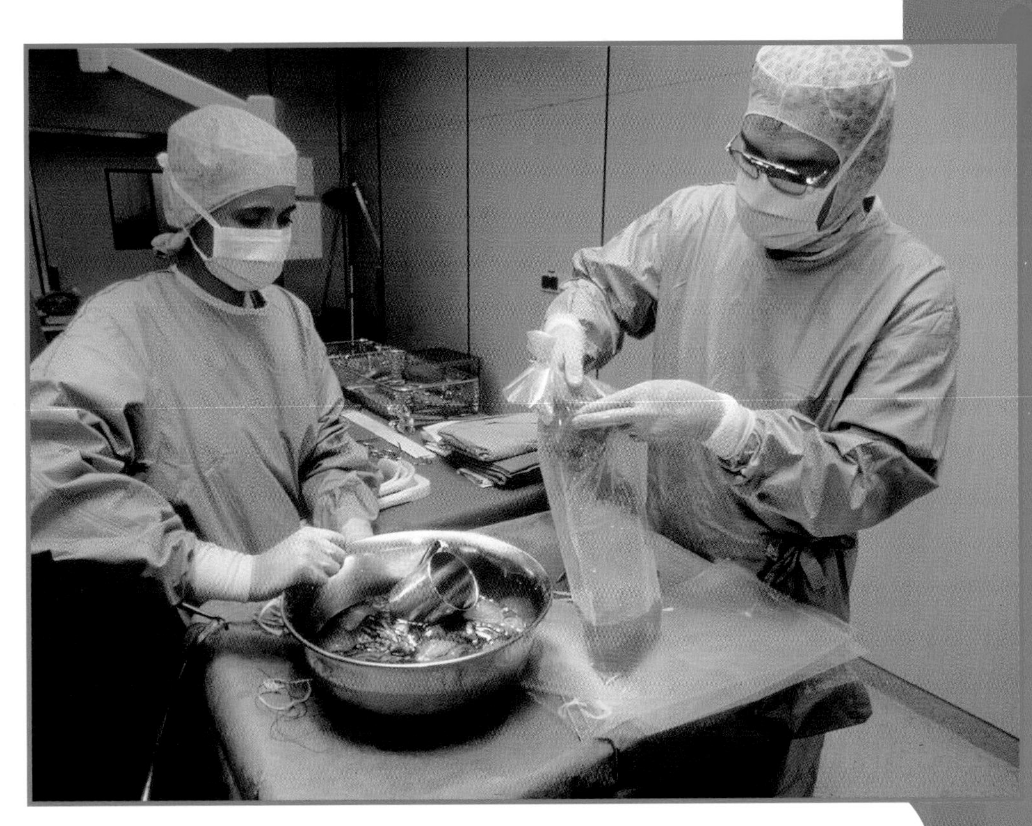

The specialized preservation fluid in which this **kidney** is being stored, along with the low storage temperatures, will make sure the kidney remains healthy while it is not functioning as part of a body.

The transplant operation

Transplanting organs always involves surgery, and all surgery involves some risk to the patient. First, the patient needs to be under an anesthetic, in a chemically induced sleep, while the operation takes place, so that he or she does not feel what is going on. It often takes a long time (several hours at least) to carry out a transplant operation. The patient has to be carefully monitored to make sure there are no problems, and the risk of problems arising increases the longer the patient is under the anesthetic.

Second, transplant surgery involves opening up the body to take out the old organ and replace it with a new one. As with all surgery, as soon as the body is opened up, it can get an **infection.** Because transplant surgery goes on for a long time and involves introducing an organ from someone else's body, the risk of infection is greatly increased.

Transplant challenges

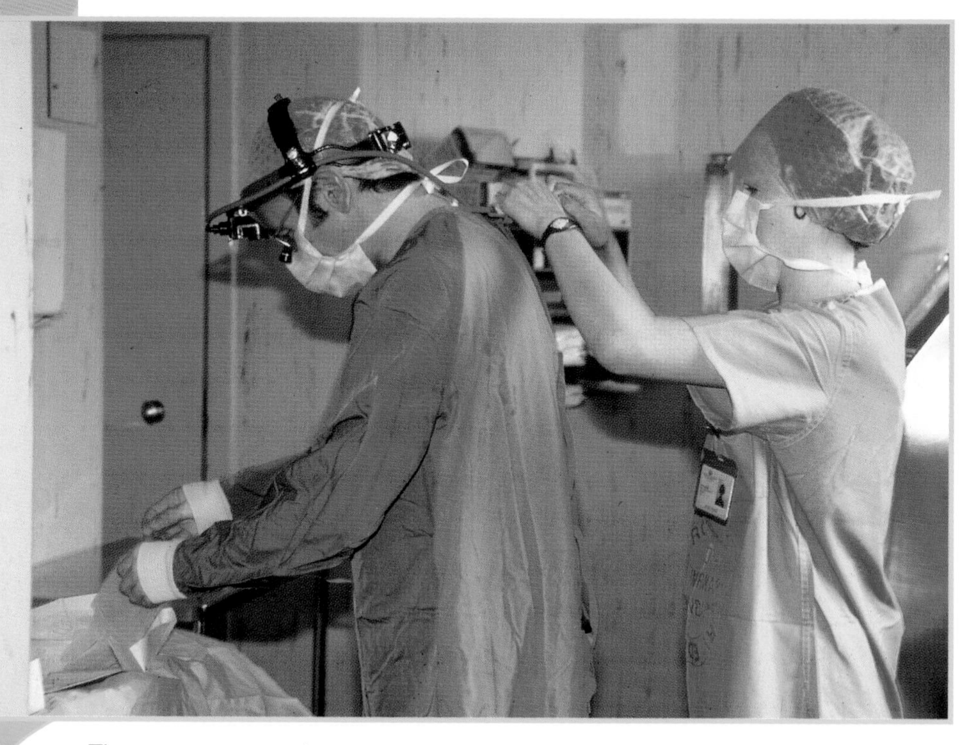

The operating team (surgeons, anesthetists, and operating-room nurses and technicians) has to maintain incredibly high standards of cleanliness. The site of the operation cannot get infected while the patient is in the operating room. Again, this is like any other operation, but because transplants tend to be very long operations, there is more opportunity for things to go wrong.

Transplanting an organ raises some particular challenges. Each organ in the body carries out specific and very important functions. In many operations, the body of the patient continues to function normally while surgery on a particular part takes place. During a transplant, entire organs are removed, so machines may have to take over their functions. This is particularly true in heart-and-lung transplants, because the body cannot function without the oxygen they provide. The patient is also often cooled down. At a low temperature the cells of the body need much less oxygen and sugar and they produce less waste. This means the cells are more likely to survive without any damage.

Another problem is making sure that the **donor** organ fits into the body of its new host. Obviously, transplants are only given when there will be a reasonable match between the size of the donor and the **recipient,** but there may still be problems. The original organ and the replacement will not be exactly the same, and neither will the blood vessels that supply them with blood. Yet these blood vessels have to be joined together in such a way that they won't leak. If the organ is much smaller or larger than the original, this can cause problems. Once the blood flow is allowed to return to the new organ, the doctors watch to see if the blood supply works and whether the transplanted organ seems to come alive in its new body.

> *The most exciting thing when you are working as a transplant surgeon is when you have put the new* ***kidney*** *in the body. You take a small, brown, cold, insignificant little thing with all the blood washed out of it from the box. You put it into your patient, connect the blood vessels—and when you remove the clamps the whole organ turns pink and expands as new life flows into it. It never stops being amazing!*
>
> Dr. Anne M. Walters, consultant renal transplant surgeon, Wessex Renal Transplant Unit, Great Britain

Anne Walters (seated in center, front row) and her team at Portsmouth, Britain, carry out kidney transplants. These are the most commonly performed transplants and the most successful.

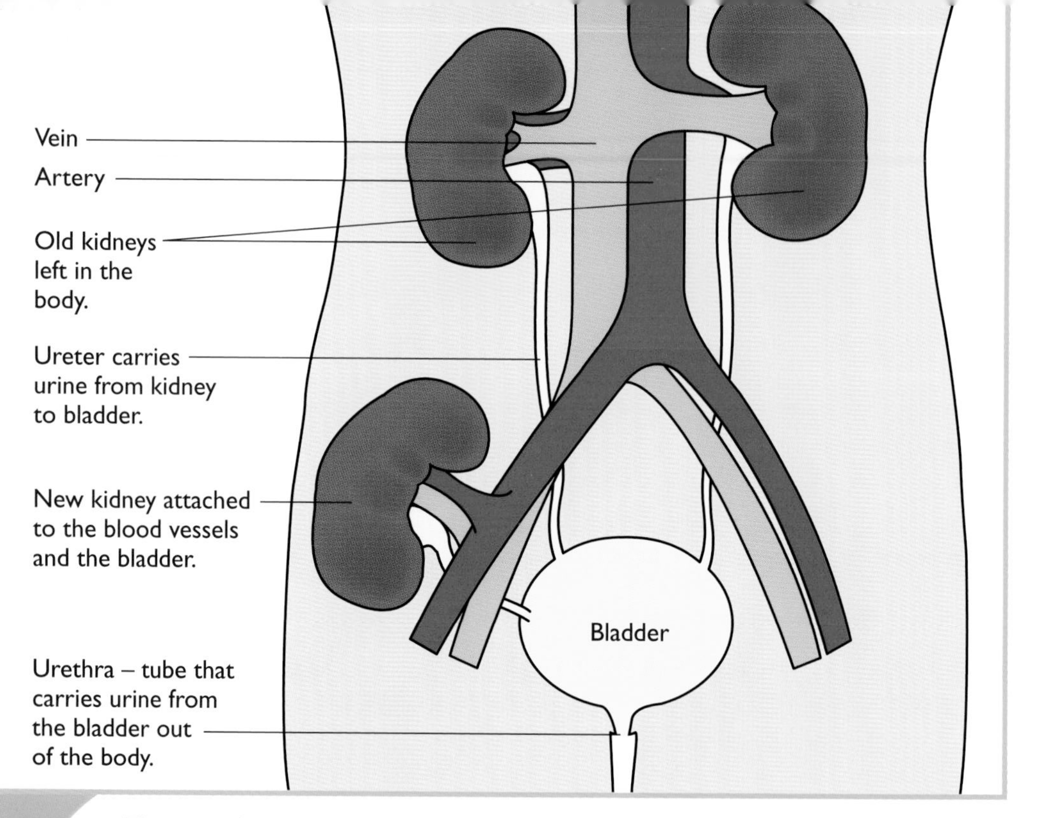

The normal procedure for a transplant leaves the failed **kidneys** in place. The new kidney is positioned lower in the body and the blood vessels of the kidney are connected to the blood vessels going to the legs, while the ureter, the tube from the kidney that carries urine away, is linked directly into the bladder.

Bigger and better

For many years, as transplant surgery was developed, single organs were transplanted to replace organs that had ceased to function. But over the years, transplant surgeons have developed a number of different techniques, some of which involve transplanting several organs at a time.

Sometimes transplants will be carried out when the patient's own organ still functions to a small extent. In these cases, "piggyback transplants" may be carried out. This means that a new organ is joined to the patient's own organ so that they work together. The new, stronger organ carries out most of the work, allowing the original organ to rest and in some cases to recover. If it does, even if the new organ is eventually **rejected** and has to be removed, the patient will remain healthy.

Doctors have become increasingly ambitious in the number of organs they transplant. Very often, the failure of one organ leads to problems in another. For example, lung disease can cause damage to the heart, or liver problems can lead to failure of parts of the digestive system. There has been a gradual increase in the transplantation of more than one organ at a time into one patient. The first successful heart-and-lung transplant was carried out by Dr. Norman Shumway and Dr. Bruce Reitz at Stanford University in 1981. Since then a number of different organ combinations have been transplanted successfully, including up to four different **abdominal organs** at a time.

> *The day after I had my transplant, I couldn't believe the effect it had on my thought processes—it was as if a fog had been lifted off my mind.*
>
> Ex-naval officer after receiving a new kidney

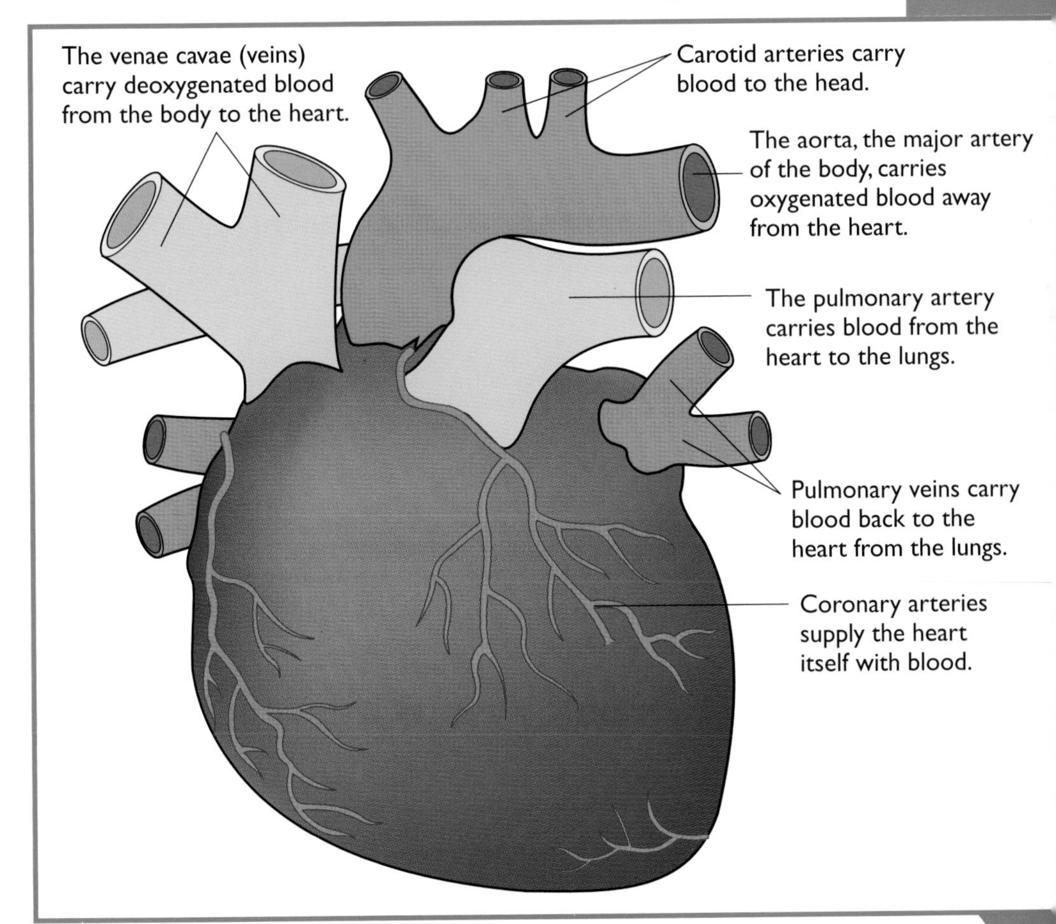

When a heart transplant is carried out, the failing heart is removed and the new organ is placed in the chest cavity to replace it. All of the massive blood vessels carrying blood back to the heart from the body and out around the body from the heart have to be reconnected so that blood doesn't leak out and make the new organ inefficient.

Domino transplants

Another new type of transplant surgery was developed in the United States in 1987. Sometimes a patient has damaged lungs but a perfectly healthy heart, such as with **genetic diseases** like cystic fibrosis. Although lung transplants can be carried out and are effective in these cases, complete heart-and-lung transplants are often more successful. This is because new connections between the heart and the lungs will not have to be made, and the two organs are the right size for each other. These transplants are known as **domino transplants** because the healthy heart of the patient who receives the new heart and lungs is then transplanted into someone else who needs a new heart. Domino transplants are still relatively rare, but they can be very successful.

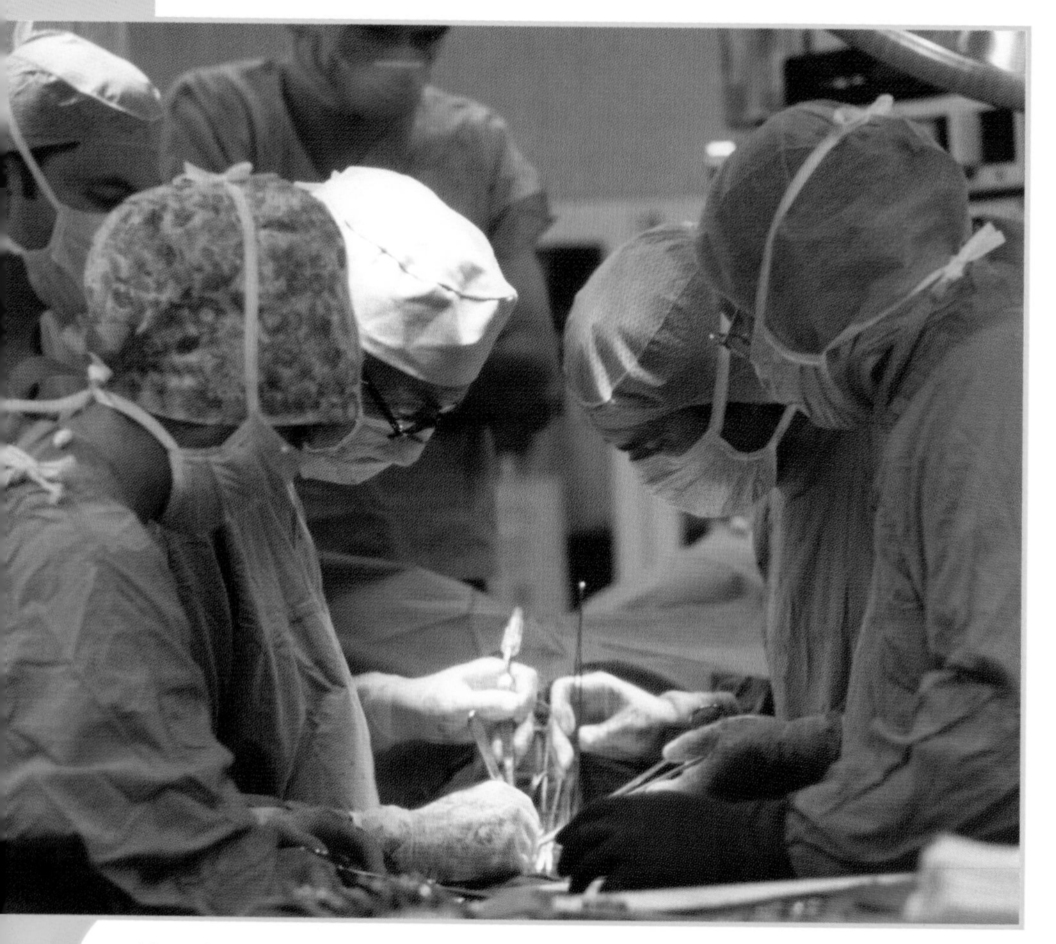

Here the transplant team at the hospital at Stanford University in California removes the diseased heart and the lungs from a patient.

Transplant coordinators

Whatever type of transplant is carried out, the success of the whole complex procedure depends heavily on the transplant coordinators.

Transplant coordinators, like Nicola Ashby (left) and Jill Pallister at the Wessex Renal Transplant Unit in Britain carry out a number of roles to keep a transplant unit running smoothly.

The coordinators are involved in supporting the **recipient** and his or her family as the patient prepares for the transplant, through the operation, and afterward as the patient recovers and learns to manage the all-important **immunosuppressant** drugs. One of their most important jobs is coordinating the transplant process once a **donor** has been found. They make sure that everyone is in the right place at the right time and that the donor organ and the recipient are in a fit condition for the surgery to go ahead. They also work with the donor families, supporting them in their grief and helping them come to terms with events. The transplant coordinators continue their support for the donor families long after the various transplants have gone ahead. They also play an important role in educating family doctors, hospital doctors, and the general public about transplant surgery.

Human blood groups—another step forward

The human **immune system** is extremely complicated and makes life very difficult for doctors wanting to transplant organs from one person to another. For example, human beings have some unique **antigens** on their red blood cells, and this divides the population into different blood groups. If some blood groups are mixed together, the antigens react with **antibodies** in the blood and cause the cells to stick together. This blocks blood vessels and can kill a patient. However, other blood groups can be mixed with no bad effects. This means that for any transplant to be successful, the blood groups of the **donor** and **recipient** must be the same or at least compatible. If not, the transplant is doomed from the start. Since the **ABO system** of categorizing human blood groups was not discovered until 1901, there was not much chance of successful transplant surgery before that time.

The immune system, which is so important in protecting the body against disease, is the worst enemy of a transplanted organ. The battle to prevent **rejection** has determined how successful transplant programs have been. For many years, the resources available to doctors were very limited and involved almost the total destruction of their patients' immune systems. This left the patients open to a wide range of **infections.** Two advances have helped to weigh the odds more strongly in favor of the patient who has received a new organ.

Making a match

All people have some antigens in common. Others are specific to a particular individual. The more closely related two individuals are, the more likely they are to have lots of antigens in common. However, completely by chance, some unrelated individuals also have very similar sets of antigens. But the only people who have exactly the same antigens on their cells are identical twins, because they both came from the same **fertilized** egg.

As human understanding of the immune system has increased, much more care has been taken with matching the **tissues** between donor and recipient. The more similar the antigens on the donor organ are to the antigens on the cells of the recipient, the better the chances of the transplant "taking" and rejection being avoided.

In Britain and Europe, there are computer databases of the tissue types of all the people waiting for organs. When a donor becomes available, the most suitable recipients can be found. Organs are then quickly taken to where they are needed. Until recently, each state in the United States tended to use organs available only within that state. Relatively recent legislation has changed this so that organs are offered to the sickest people with the best tissue match, rather than to the nearest needy patient. Unfortunately for patients, some states are contesting this to protect the interests of their own residents.

Research in the United States has shown that out of 7,614 people who got a perfect tissue-match transplant, 52 percent of the organs were still working ten years later. In contrast, out of a group of 81,364 patients who had less-than-perfect matches, only 32 percent of the organs were still working ten years later. So a good match makes a lot of difference.

Making sure that recipients get tissue-matching organs often involves high-speed flights across great distances to get the right organ to the right patient.

Preventing rejection with drugs

In 1969, scientists in the United States and Norway discovered a **fungus** that was to have far-reaching effects on the success of transplant surgery in the future. In 1972, Jean Borel, working in Switzerland, found that a chemical called **cyclosporine,** which could be isolated from the fungus, had **immunosuppressant** properties. In other words, it suppressed the **immune system's** reaction. By 1980, this "wonder **molecule**" had been **synthesized** for the first time, and by 1983, it was approved for commercial and clinical use. When patients take cyclosporine after a transplant, the risk of **rejection** is greatly reduced because the activity of the immune system is lowered.

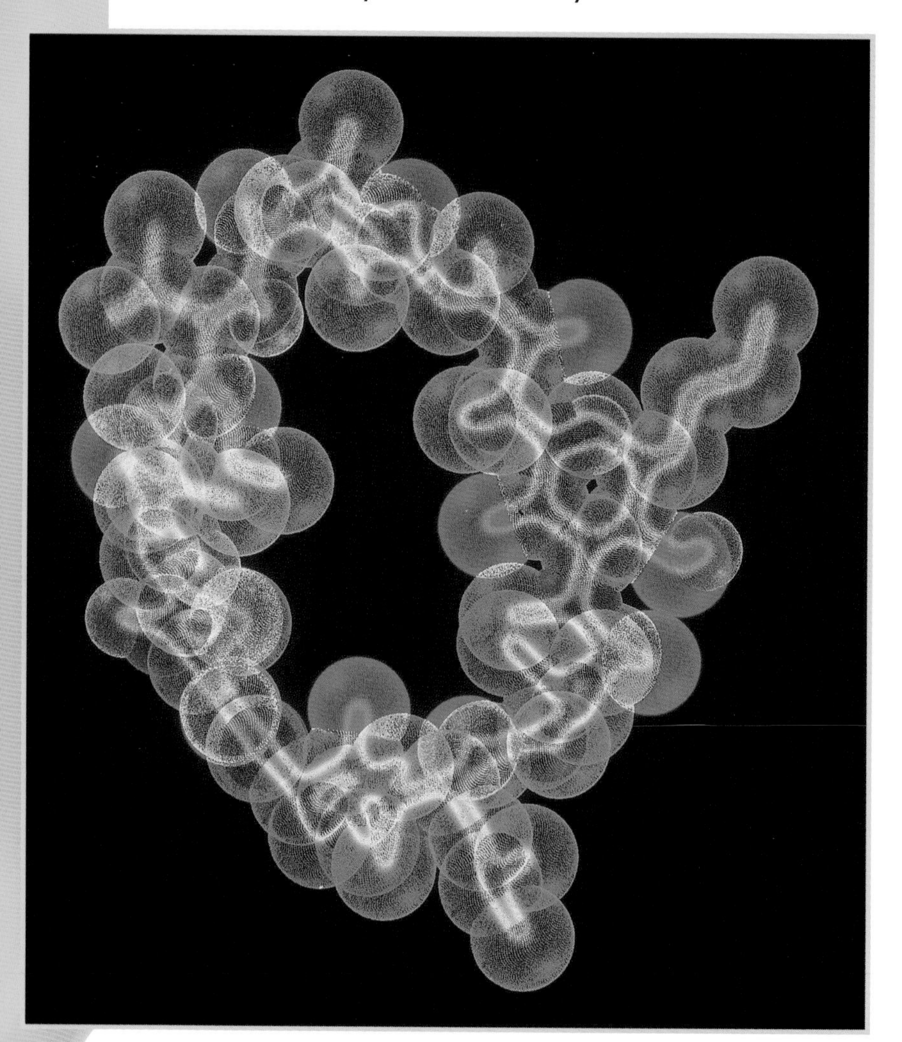

A molecule of cyclosporine, the amazing new immuno-suppressant drug that has enabled thousands of people to benefit from an organ transplant without rejection problems.

Cyclosporine, particularly when used in partnership with other drugs such as some **steroids,** has had a major impact on the numbers of people having successful transplants. However, transplant patients have to take their immunosuppressant drugs for the rest of their lives, because the body would never get used to the new organ and accept it. The main downside of drugs like this is that they suppress the whole immune system. People taking immunosuppressant drugs are more likely to develop **infections.** Because everyone is aware of this, transplant patients are carefully monitored and given other medicines to help them if they develop an infectious illness.

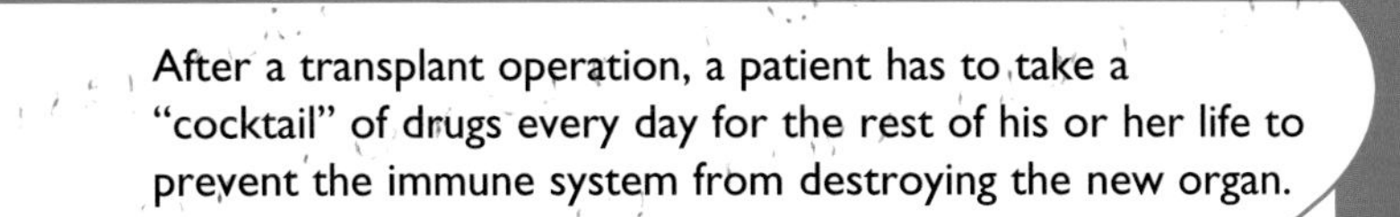

After a transplant operation, a patient has to take a "cocktail" of drugs every day for the rest of his or her life to prevent the immune system from destroying the new organ.

In the last ten years, many new drugs have been developed to help guard against rejection. Some have replaced cyclosporine, while others are used alongside it. Pharmacologists (people who study the science of drugs) are great allies of transplant surgeons in the war against rejection.

Life from Death

When someone has an organ that is failing, the obvious solution is to replace it with a new one. There is one huge problem with this, however. Where is the new organ going to come from?

The most common source of **donor** organs are people who have died. Road accidents kill about 40,000 people a year in the United States alone. Many of those killed are relatively young and healthy apart from the injuries—often to the brain—that kill them. Some people die from an unexpected hemorrhage (massive bleeding) in the brain or a **heart attack.** Whenever a healthy person meets a sudden, unexpected death, most of their organs will be in perfectly good condition. These organs can be given to someone else who may be dying because his or her heart, **kidneys,** liver, or another organ can no longer function.

Every day, people leave their homes to go to work, to school, or out with friends and unfortunately never return. The roads claim many lives every week, and many people have to come to terms with sudden and totally unexpected losses.

Granting permission

Many people die without having left written permission for their organs to be given to someone else. It is illegal for doctors to remove organs from a dead body for the purpose of transplantation without permission. If organs are to be used for transplantation, the donor must be kept on a life-support machine, even after the donor is clinically dead (all brain activity is lost). The machine pumps blood around his or her body and keeps the organs supplied with oxygen to keep them functioning. If the body functions for even a short time without oxygen, the organs will be damaged and useless to anyone else. The machine takes over the functions of the heart and the lungs, getting oxygen into the blood, pumping it around the body, and removing **carbon dioxide.**

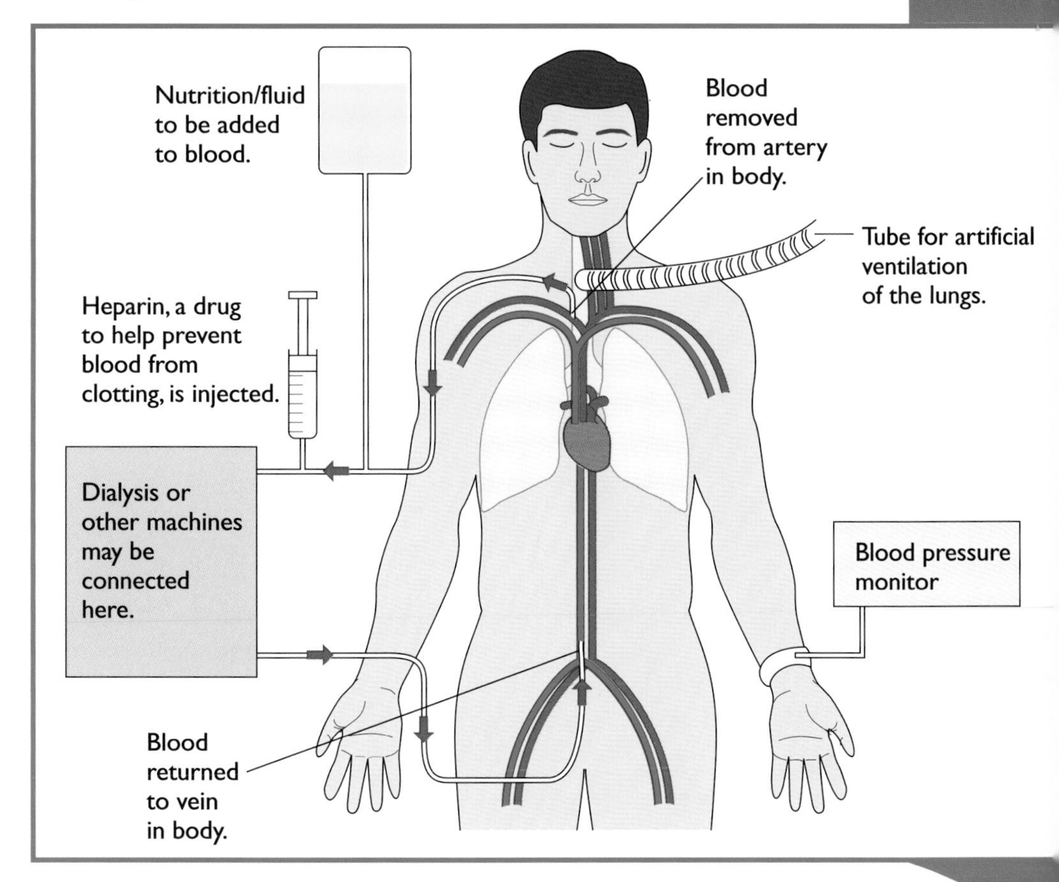

When an accident victim or someone who has suffered some type of medical catastrophe is brought into the hospital, they will be put on a life-support machine if it is needed. This gives doctors the opportunity to assess the patient to see if there is any chance of his or her survival. It also keeps the organs, such as the liver and kidneys, functioning. If the patient's organs are to be used for transplantation, the patient will be kept on the machine even after he or she is found to be clinically dead, until the organs are removed.

When is death?

Doctors can only use a person's organs for transplantation if that person is dead. But how do we know when someone is dead and has no hope of recovery? In past years, people were judged to be dead when their hearts stopped beating and they stopped breathing. Many people still think of death in this way. But in the case of sudden death, whether due to accidents or medical emergencies, machines can maintain the working of the body. In some cases, the heart keeps functioning at the level of a very basic reflex, a rapid nervous response that does not involve the **central nervous system.** In these cases, doctors have to look elsewhere for a definition of death. A patient is defined as being dead when the brain stem, the very lowest region of the brain, is dead. Once the basic regions of the brain stop functioning, the patient has no awareness, no thought, and no life except that given by machines. Once a patient is certified as brain-stem dead—a process that takes a long time and several doctors—then the possibility of using the organs for transplantation becomes real.

A dreadful situation

When a patient is certified as dead, it is a terrible time for everyone concerned. Doctors are faced with a dreadful situation. If they ask the relatives, who are stunned, shocked, and grieving, for permission to use the organs of their loved one for transplantation, then the doctors may add to the distress of the relatives. If they do not ask, then they are losing the chance of prolonging the lives of several people waiting desperately for an organ transplant. If the organs are to be used for successful transplants, there is no time to lose.

For the relatives, this is a hard decision to make at a horrible time, and if they have not thought about it before, then they may feel unable to "give away" part of their loved one's body. If the potential **donor** is on a life-support machine, then they will still be warm, appear to be breathing, and will look as if they are simply asleep, making it even harder for relatives to accept that death has occurred. If permission to use the organs is refused, the life-support machine will be switched off when it seems right to the family, usually after a few hours.

The donor card

There is one thing that can make this situation easier for everyone concerned. In countries like Great Britain, the United States, and Australia, there is a system of organ donor cards. Healthy, living people can decide that if anything should happen to them, then they would like their organs to be used to give life to other people. To show that this is their choice, they carry an organ donor card with them. If they are involved in an accident or become seriously ill and die, the doctors know immediately that the organs are available for transplantation. Very often, people have also discussed this with their relatives, so that the family already knows their wishes.

I request that after my death

*A. my *kidneys, *corneas, *heart, *lungs, *liver, *pancreas be used for transplantation, or

*B. any part of my body be used for the treatment of others

*(DELETE AS APPROPRIATE)

Signature__________ Date__________

Full name__________
(BLOCK CAPITALS)

In the event of my death, if possible contact:

Name__________ Tel.__________

If people are carrying organ donor cards when they die, doctors know that they can use their organs for transplantation. This allows them to have the greatest chance of being successful donors. In the U.S., many states give people the option of having an organ donor card on the back of their driver's license, and in Britain, there is a computer database of registered organ donors so they no longer need to carry a donor card.

Deciding to be a donor

When someone expresses a wish to be an organ **donor** after his or her death, it makes the situation much easier if they do die suddenly. However, persuading people to become potential donors and carry a donor card is difficult. People often don't want to think about the possibility of their own death. Many other people are full of good intentions but simply do not get around to picking up a donor card. Some countries now have a system where everyone is automatically assumed to be a potential organ donor. Anyone who does not want to give their organs has to choose to not participate in this system. This has greatly increased the number of organs available for transplantation in those countries where it has been tried, such as Belgium.

In many states of the U.S., laws require doctors to ask the families of all potential donors if they will allow donation. This means that they cannot be accused of being insensitive at a difficult time, because they are simply obeying the law. For many other families, however, the opportunity to donate organs from their loved one's body is seen as a way of bringing something positive out of a terrible situation.

> *It is a very, very noble act—and human beings are capable of very noble acts. . . . They can help seven or eight other people live who are about to die—they [the family] think that something good can come out of it.*
>
> Professor Sir Magdi Yacoub, senior transplant surgeon at Harefield Hospital, Britain

> *If anything ever happens to me I want my organs to go to someone else.*
>
> Scott Dudley (American teenager), not long before he was killed in an accident with a gun. His organs gave two people their sight (using the corneas from his eyes), and four lives were saved with his heart, **kidneys,** liver, and pancreas.

Living donors

While most transplants are carried out using organs removed after death, not all organ donors are dead. Living donors are an increasingly important group. Usually, living donors are members of the same family as the person who is suffering from organ failure.

There is obviously a limit to the number and type of organs that can be given by a living donor. The most commonly donated organs are kidneys, because everyone has two of them. An individual can live perfectly well with just one kidney. However, the donor is obviously

Parents, brothers, sisters, uncles, aunts, or cousins (blood relatives) have a much higher chance of providing good tissue matches than unrelated donors do. Husbands and wives have also sometimes been able to act as donors for each other. Above, in Seattle, Washington, Olufeyi Ogunyemi stands with her brother, who donated **bone marrow** to help Olufeyi.

more at risk if he or she ever has kidney problems. The donor will have lost his or her "spare." The liver, too, or at least part of it, can be donated. Although each person has only one liver, it is a large organ that regrows at a very rapid rate. Part of the liver can be removed from a living donor, and blood vessels from this **tissue** can be joined to the blood vessels supplying the **recipient's** liver. The liver tissue will regenerate in both the donor and the recipient very quickly, and the transplant will take over the function of the damaged or destroyed liver.

Most living donors freely give their organ either to someone they love or to someone they do not know but who has appealed for an organ as a matter of urgency. However, in some parts of the world where there is great poverty, such as India, there have been many instances of people selling their organs, particularly kidneys, for use in transplantation. Many groups find this unacceptable, particularly if people are pressured to do it. It seems wrong that people should compromise their own health by donating an organ simply for money.

Ethics and issues

When it comes to doing something as amazing as taking an organ out of one person, living or dead, and putting it inside the body of another person, there are bound to be all sorts of concerns.

Some people simply cannot come to terms with the idea of part of one person being used inside another, and they feel that they could never be organ **donors.** Other people find the idea of the body of someone they love being divided up and organs being removed very hard to accept, particularly if they only think about it when someone very close to them has died unexpectedly. Added to this, there are occasional "scare stories" in the press of people taking on another personality after a transplant operation, particularly heart transplants. Other people feel that it would be against their religion.

In fact, most religions have no problem with organ donation. The Christian religions all see organ donation, either from a dead or living donor, as an act of compassion and giving to save life. All churches share concern when the donor is dead, feeling that the body should be treated with respect and that organ donation should not be done for money. Within these constraints, transplant surgery is seen as a good and beneficial form of medicine.

> *Organ donation is an* ***altruistic*** *act which is motivated by compassion and a sense of social responsibility. Christians should, generally, be encouraged to reflect on how they can help those in need, even after death.*
>
> Right Reverend Michael Nazir-Ali, Bishop of Rochester, England

The teachings of Islam also support organ donation. Saving lives is very important to Muslims, and they are both allowed to accept organ donation and to act as organ donors themselves. While both donor and **recipient** ideally would be Muslim, in practice saving all life is seen as important.

> *. . . And if anyone saved a life it would be as if he saved the life of the whole people . . .*
>
> Koran, chapter 5, verse 32

Many other religious groups also support transplantation. Hindus, Sikhs, and Buddhists all see organ donation as being totally acceptable and more than that, a positive and generous gesture.

> *Buddhists totally agree with organ donation. It is quite acceptable.*
>
> Ven Pidiville Piyatissa,
> Sri Lankan-born Buddhist monk

Even the Jehovah's Witnesses, well known for their refusal to accept blood transfusions, are allowed to receive organ transplants if the surgery is carried out without the use of transfusions. "Bloodless surgery" has been developed to allow this to take place. This involves chilling the whole body to very low temperatures to reduce any bleeding and using special fluids that can carry oxygen to bathe the **tissues,** instead of using blood products.

There is remarkable agreement from all religions about how honorable and unselfish organ donation is.

Lucy's Story

Organ transplantation has always been an uncertain science. Even today, with all our knowledge and technology, transplants can fail immediately after they have been carried out or years later. This uncertainty is hard for doctors who cannot predict which transplants will be successful and which will not. It is much harder for the patients and their families, who have to live with that uncertainty every single day. The story of Lucy Sheehan shows what it is like to be on the receiving end of transplant surgery.

The first signs

On December 11, 1988, Amanda and James Sheehan welcomed their sixth child into the world. Lucy was an alert and endearing baby, but she remained rather small. In fact, she had regular medical checkups because she was growing so slowly. However, by the time Lucy was two years old, she was making up the lost ground rapidly, and her mother took her for what she hoped might be one of her last checkups. Completely unexpectedly, Dr. Ahmed Mukhtar felt that Lucy's liver was enlarged when he examined her, and he decided to give her a **scan** just to make sure all was well. The results of the scan were

When Lucy (seen here on the left, with her older sister) was two, she appeared to be a normal, lively toddler. But she had to go into the hospital and have a whole battery of tests to find out what was going on inside her liver.

frightening. Lucy's liver was tough and scarred. It looked as if she had **cirrhosis** of the liver, a disease that is commonly found in alcoholics.

The family was quickly referred to King's College Hospital in London, one of the top centers for research into liver disease in Britain and Europe.

> *Most children with liver disease look ill and yellow—they have jaundice —but Lucy didn't, she didn't look ill at all. That made it very hard for us to believe that anything was wrong with her—it was all such a shock.*
>
> Amanda Sheehan, Lucy's mother

The whole process of going to the hospital and having tests distressed Lucy greatly, but the results that came back showed that the scan had been right. Lucy really did have cirrhosis of the liver, but the doctors simply didn't know why. Somewhere, the complex chemistry taking place in Lucy's liver had gone wrong, but in a way that the doctors had never been seen before. Because Lucy was still feeling so well, they decided that the best thing to do was keep a close watch on her. Amanda and James were told to take her home and bring her to the hospital for regular checkups every three months.

Lucy with a doctor from King's College Hospital in 1992. Although the Sheehan family didn't know it when they first took Lucy for liver tests, this famous hospital was going to play a major part in their lives for many years to come.

A grim reality

Once Lucy came back from her tests, life began to return to normal in the Sheehan family. With six children—Penny, Philip, Oliver, Nicholas, Hannah, and Lucy—life was pretty hectic and there wasn't much time to worry about what might happen at the next checkup. But it was only two weeks later when the doctors gave Amanda some very bad news. More results from Lucy's tests had shown something abnormal. They were asked to come back to the hospital as soon as possible. The doctors suspected that Lucy might have **cancer** of the liver, but it would take more time and tests before they could be sure. By the summer, when Lucy was two and a half, the doctors finally arrived at a decision. Lucy not only had **cirrhosis** of the liver. She also had cells that were precancerous (becoming cancerous). She needed a liver transplant as soon as possible. The longer she waited, the more likely it was that cancer would develop and spread beyond the liver. Without a transplant, the doctors said she had about two years to live. In September 1991, Lucy officially went on the list of children waiting for a liver transplant.

> *It was like being on a terrifying emotional roller-coaster ride. We never knew what we would have to deal with next. To be told that your two-year-old child might not live to be four—we just went completely cold.*
>
> Amanda Sheehan, Lucy's mother

The long wait

Ideally, Lucy needed a transplant right away, but **donor** organs often are simply not available when they are needed. Yet the family knew that the longer they waited, the faster Lucy's chances of survival would continue to slip away. The constant hospital visits were taking a toll on everyone. James, Lucy's father, ran the family business, so every time he took time off work he was not earning money. Lucy's brothers and sisters needed time and attention, too. The family had to pay someone to help look after the other children when Lucy and her mother made their many trips to the hospital.

Lucy's illness was affecting the whole family. Running a household for eight people takes a lot of money, especially when paying for extra help. All of the children were worried and missed their mother and Lucy whenever they were away at the hospital. There was no sign of a donor organ becoming available, so when Amanda had the chance to appear on national television, she took advantage and made an appeal for people to think about donating organs if their loved ones died.

Amanda and Lucy appeared on several television programs where Amanda appealed for donor organs to be made available and helped explain what hardships this situation places on the whole family. Lucy received her transplant two days after this TV appearance in June, 1992.

As a result of their television appearance, the family received a lot of support. People ran in marathons and organized collections to help them financially. Two weeks later, they received a call from the hospital saying a donor organ was available. Lucy was prepared for surgery, and her family said good-bye. However, they knew that another little girl in a worse situation than Lucy's was also being prepared for surgery. The surgeons opened her up first. If the other girl had cancer that had already spread, it would not have been worth transplanting the donor liver into her body. However, although her liver was cancerous, there was no sign of the disease spreading. The other girl's need was greater, so she got the liver. Lucy and her family had to keep waiting.

The transplant

More time went by without an organ becoming available. After eight months, Amanda and Lucy went on television again to raise the profile of people needing transplants and to ask people to think about becoming organ **donors.** In that week alone, as a direct result of the TV appeal, enough donor organs were made available to enable nine children to have transplant operations. One of those children was Lucy.

On June 13, 1992, as the family was having a party to celebrate Hannah's birthday, the call came through to say a donor organ had been found. The whole family piled into the car and drove to King's College Hospital, with Lucy still in her party dress. Her brothers and sisters said good-bye to her that night, knowing they might not see her alive again. On June 14, the operation went ahead. James took the other children home while Amanda waited at the hospital for the eight hours that Lucy was in the operating room. Lucy was given one lobe (section) of the liver of an older child (the liver normally consists of two lobes).

When Lucy emerged from the operation, she was put into intensive care, but she only stayed there for 24 hours. She was soon pulling her own ventilation tubes out. At three and a half, Lucy couldn't really understand why she had come to the hospital feeling fine and now felt so very poorly. For several weeks, she refused to eat and had to be fed through a tube. She needed nine different medicines daily to prevent her body from rejecting the new liver. After six weeks in the hospital, she went home, only to have her body start to reject the liver. Shaking, with a high temperature, she was rushed back into the hospital as an emergency case. The doctors were not surprised. Most children who receive a new organ reject it at first. But once the **rejection** was under control, Lucy went home again and this time she recovered well, eating normally and getting back her zest for life.

The intervals between her checkups got longer and longer as her new liver continued to work well. It wasn't all smooth sailing, though. In the first two years after her transplant, Lucy had a number of **infections,** including mononucleosis. This illness attacks the glands of the **immune system** and causes extreme fatigue. The infections caused major problems because of the **immunosuppressant** drugs she had to take, which already were suppressing Lucy's immune system. But Lucy and her family just kept going and their dedication paid off. Lucy is still fit and well today.

The liver that saved Lucy's life was donated by the family of a twelve-year-old boy who died during an operation on a tumor (an uncontrolled growth of cells) in his brain. No one had expected him to die, and doctors did not ask his stunned parents for permission to use their son's organs. It was the parents themselves who volunteered their son as a donor, in the midst of their own horrible loss. Their generosity allowed Lucy to live.

> *I'm so grateful to my donor. My liver doesn't feel different or strange—it just feels like part of me. I feel completely normal.*
>
> Lucy Sheehan, transplant patient

Lucy Sheehan is now a healthy, active teenager. She has had her new liver for nine years and only has to take a very low dose of two medicines, including **cyclosporine,** each day. She goes to school and joins in all the same activities as her friends and relatives. She is a real transplant success story.

Pushing the Boundaries

Every 27 minutes, someone somewhere in the world receives an organ transplant. But every two hours and 24 minutes, someone dies waiting for an organ **donor** to turn up. There are simply not enough donor organs available for all the people who need them, and the problem seems to be getting worse rather than better. As surgical techniques and **immunosuppressant** drugs have improved, transplant surgery is seen as the answer to more and more medical problems. At the same time, the introduction of seat-belt laws, a reduction in drinking and driving, and improved car safety standards have resulted in fewer people being killed in road accidents. Doctors are able to save the lives of more people who are rushed into hospitals. These improvements are welcomed by everyone, but the inevitable side effect is a reduction in the amount of potential organ donors.

Organs are released from only about 20 percent of potential donors. The supply of donor organs from people who have died will never match the number of people needing transplants, no matter how much awareness is raised about the importance of organ transplantation and the need for donors. Living donors are being used increasingly, but they are also a very limited resource. It is because of this mismatch of supply and demand that research into alternative ways of providing organs for transplantation has been ongoing.

Xenotransplantation

One area of research that has received a great deal of media attention and funding is **xenotransplantation.** This is the transplantation of organs from other species of animals into humans. Xenotransplantation is not actually a new science. In 1906, a French surgeon, Mathieu Jaboulay, implanted a pig's **kidney** into one woman and a goat's liver into another. Neither woman survived. However, in recent years, scientists began to think that the use of xenotransplants could solve two of the biggest problems of transplant surgery, the shortage of donor organs and the problems of **rejection.**

Most of the research into using animals as a source of organs for human transplants has been done using baboons and pigs. In 1964, six patients received baboon kidneys; in 1984, a baboon heart was transplanted into a baby girl; and in 1992, two patients received baboon livers. All of the patients died within weeks of their operations, but they did not die because they had rejected their new organs. The high dosages of immunosuppressant drugs they needed to take left them highly vulnerable to **infections,** and they died because of these. Furthermore, baboons are not an ideal source of organs because they reproduce very slowly, having only one baby at a time. They also carry many viruses that could be passed on to the human **recipient.** Many people also have **ethical** objections to using baboons as "donors." In their looks, behaviors, and biology, they are similar to humans. Objections arise because when animals are used as a source of organs for human transplants, the animals are always killed.

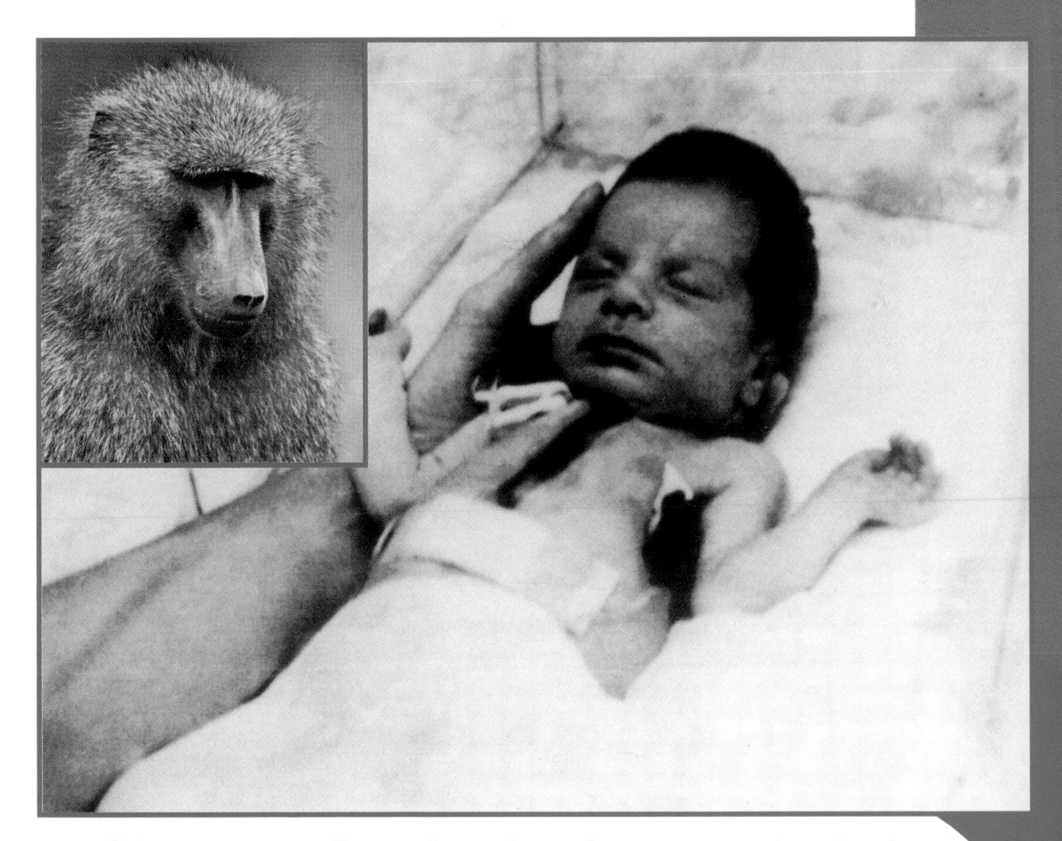

Baboons are genetically very close to human beings, so researchers thought that rejection problems would probably be relatively small. Physically, the baboon organs would also fit easily into a person. In 1984, this little girl, known in the press as "Baby Faye," received a baboon's heart to try to keep her alive. The baboon's heart worked in her body for twenty days, but she died of infection before a suitable human donor was found.

What about a pig's heart?

As possible organ sources, pigs have been the main focus of research. Despite the difference in body shape, the anatomy of a pig is amazingly similar to a human's. Pigs also carry fewer viruses than baboons, are much easier to breed, and produce lots of piglets every time they give birth. There are also fewer moral objections to using pigs because they are killed for food anyway. The hope among researchers is that, using the techniques of **genetic engineering,** pigs may be modified so they produce hearts, livers, **kidneys,** and other organs that carry neutral human **antigens.** This would mean the new organs would not be recognized by the human **recipient** as foreign **tissue.** The hope is that genetically modified pigs raised in a sterile environment might provide a virtually unlimited supply of disease-free "human" organs for transplants. The recipients would also need little or no **immunosuppressant** drugs, as the new organs would be recognized by their **immune systems** as "human."

Genetically modified pigs to be used for organ transplants would not be able to live in a natural environment like this. They would need to be reared in a very sterile, biomedical environment, and this raises animal-welfare issues. Would it be fair to treat these intelligent animals in this way?

In January 2002, scientists working at the University of Missouri announced that they had produced genetically modified pigs that could one day be used as safe sources for organs to transplant into humans. The scientists also said that their pigs had certain genetic characteristics that would make the pig organs less likely to be **rejected** by humans after transplants. Another U.S. group, PPL Therapeutics, announced similar findings in January. Both groups believed that with more research, they could soon be producing pig hearts and kidneys that the human immune system would not reject.

Advantages and disadvantages

What are the big advantages of using animals to provide organs for human beings? Obviously, patients would never again die waiting for a **donor** organ. There would always be suitable organs available, and the problem of rejection could be solved. It sounds like a wonderful solution to the problem. So what are the drawbacks of **xenotransplantation?** There are a number of **ethical** objections. For example, animals cannot give consent for the use of their organs. For this reason, they cannot be referred to as donors. They are organ sources. Also, the animals would have to be kept in very unnatural, sterile conditions.

The other major problem is the risk of disease. Like all animals, including ourselves, baboons and pigs carry a wide range of viruses, although pigs have fewer than baboons. Many of these are relatively harmless in the baboon or the pig, but any of them could cause a fatal disease in a human. An example is the virus that causes **AIDS.** This is a relatively harmless virus in monkeys but it has devastating effects in people. No one knows if xenotransplants would bring new and deadly diseases into the human race, but it is a very big risk to take.

A large amount of money has been invested in research on xenotransplantation, and pigs carrying human genes have been bred in Britain and elsewhere. However, the general opinion increasingly seems to be that xenotransplantation will not be the answer, that there are too many problems to be overcome in xenotransplantation, and that other areas of research will come up with the best solution for the shortage of donor organs.

> *There has been a lot of scientific hype, leading people to believe that successful animal transplants are just around the corner. But now the [Regulatory Authority] is saying that this is not the case and there are serious concerns about safety. . . .*
>
> Sarah Kite, British Union for the Abolition of Vivisection

Research—The Cutting Edge

The number of people waiting for an organ transplant around the world is large, and it is growing. About 44,000 Americans are on the waiting lists, yet only 18,270 operations were carried out in the year 2000. In Britain, there are almost 7,000 people waiting for transplants, and in Australia, the numbers are similar. It was hoped that **xenotransplantation** would provide a ready supply of organs. At the same time as those hopes faded, new discoveries were being made that may well be the answer to the organ shortage in the future.

The pluripotent stem cell

Embryonic stem cells divide and form the specialized cells of the body that make up the various **tissues** and organs. When an egg and sperm fuse to form an **embryo,** those early cells will eventually give rise to every type of cell in the adult human body. By the stage at which the embryo implants in the mother's **uterus,** it has become a hollow ball of cells. The inner cells of this ball are what is known as pluripotent. These cells will eventually form most, but not all, of the baby's cells. These pluripotent stem cells

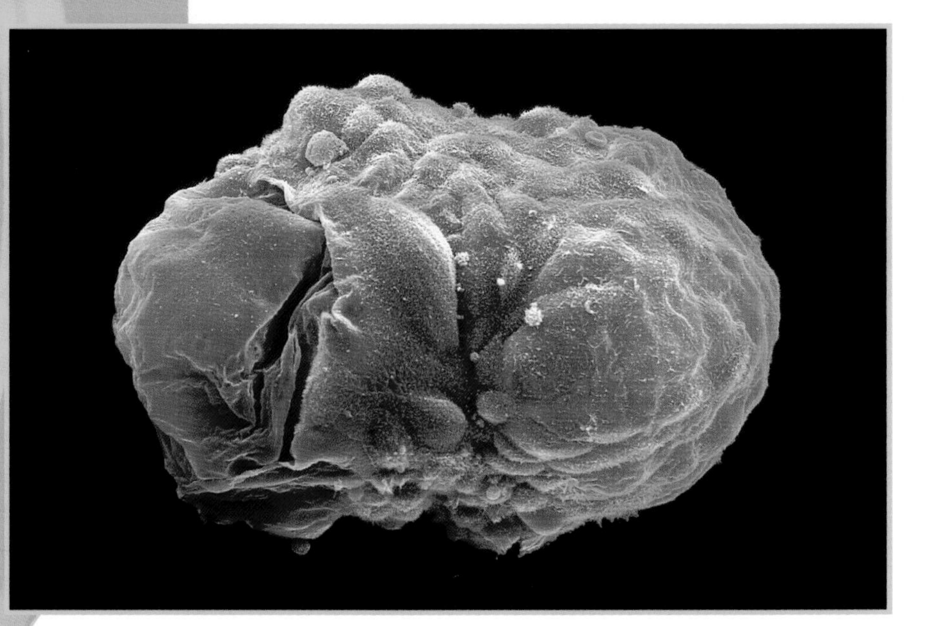

This is a very early human embryo. In the right conditions in the uterus, these few cells can form all of the organs of the human body. Now, scientists may be able to harness and use that potential.

get even more specialized as the embryo develops, forming, for example, blood stem cells, which give rise to blood cells, and skin stem cells, which give rise to skin cells.

In 1998, in a breakthrough that caused ripples of excitement through the scientific and medical world, two American scientists managed to **culture** human embryonic stem cells that were still pluripotent. Dr. James Thomson and his research team at the University of Wisconsin maintained a culture of human embryonic stem cells for several months. They originally got the cells from spare embryos that had been produced during **in vitro fertilization** treatments. Couples had donated their spare embryos for scientific research, rather than having them destroyed.

At the same time, Dr. John Gearhart and his group at Johns Hopkins University were also culturing human embryonic stem cells from a slightly different part of the embryo. The cells used by Gearhart came from fetuses that had been aborted after five to nine weeks of development.

John Gearhart and his team, working at Johns Hopkins University (above), published their findings on embryonic stem cells just four days after James Thomson, and both groups are credited with this groundbreaking discovery.

Why so much excitement?

The culturing of embryonic stem cells caused a major stir. In theory at least, the pluripotent cells could be encouraged to grow into almost any different type of cell needed in the body. They could provide an amazing variety of cures for diseases and other medical problems. For example, they could provide new nerve cells for people with brain disorders or spinal injuries, new heart-muscle cells to repair hearts damaged by **heart attacks,** and new and effective treatments for **strokes,** burns, and **arthritis.** For those people waiting desperately for a transplant, the hope is that it may be possible to produce whole new organs by growing the stem cells in the right conditions. This means there may be a potentially limitless source of **donor** organs. It could also revolutionize the treatment of many other diseases and change the testing of drugs, reducing the need for animal experiments.

At the moment, no one is quite sure just how the cells in an embryo are switched on or off to form particular types of tissue, such as **kidney** rather than liver or liver rather than heart. As the answers to these questions are found, the potential for a limitless supply of new organs could develop. Not only that, but the problem of **rejection** could be solved. The **immune system** does not attack and destroy a developing **embryo,** even though it has different **antigens** on its cells than the mother. Perhaps new cells or organs created from embryonic stem cells will enjoy this same protection.

The ethical obstacle

The major **ethical** problem with research into pluripotent cells is that these cells come either from aborted embryos or from "spare" embryos in fertility-treatment facilities. There are many people, including many religious groups, who feel it is wrong to use a potential human being as a source of material in this way. It is also argued that the embryo cannot give permission, so it is a violation of the embryo's human rights to use it.

The research is so controversial that federal government funding was stopped for a time in the United States until the situation could be discussed in detail. As of August 9, 2001, the U.S. government has been funding research that uses human pluripotent cells. Federal funding is only allowed for research on cells that were in existence before August 9, so no more cells can be obtained from "spare" or aborted embryos. These restrictions do not apply to privately funded U.S. research companies that are conducting research on pluripotent cells.

The use of embryonic stem cells from the umbilical cord (the cord that joins the developing baby to the mother's **placenta** in the **uterus**) may help to overcome some of the reservations. It may become possible to store stem cells from every newborn baby, so the cells could be used if the baby should need them later in life.

Scientists are also finding some stem cells in adults that appear to have the ability to grow into several different types of tissue. There seem to be more limitations with adult stem cells than with embryonic ones. The adult stem cells found so far can develop into only a few cell types. However, this is another technique that could avoid both **rejection** problems and the controversial use of embryonic tissue.

Most people remain excited by the possibilities of embryonic stem cells in transplantation and other areas. Only time will tell just how many of these early hopes will be fulfilled.

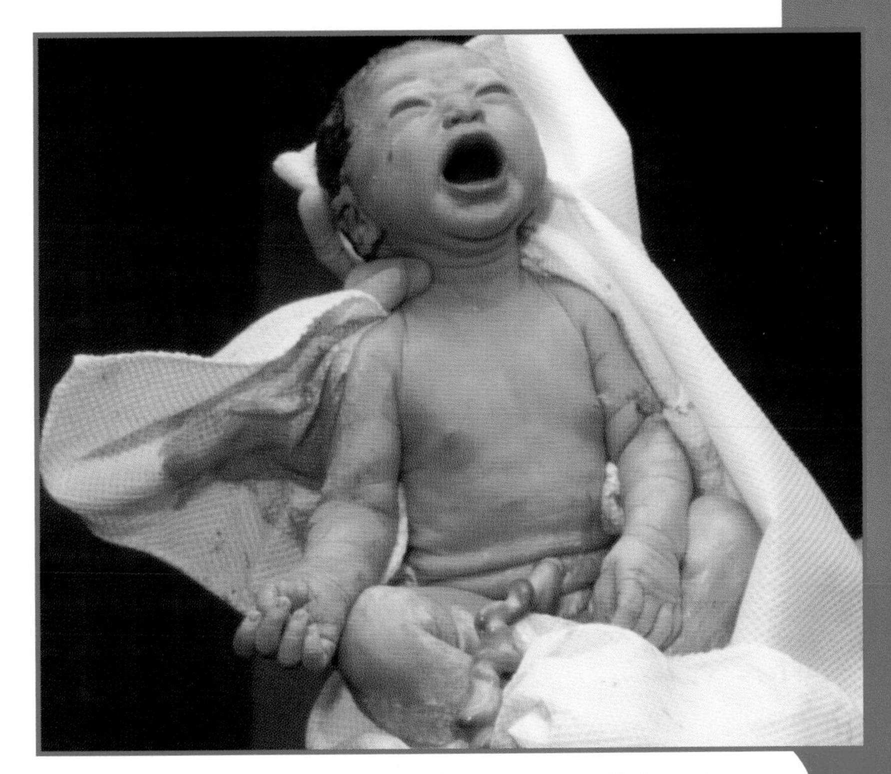

It may be possible to harvest embryonic stem cells from the umbilical cords of newborn babies. This would avoid the use of tissue from early embryos and overcome ethical problems.

Into the Future

The field of organ transplantation is exciting and always advancing. Surgeons are always looking for new techniques that will make transplants more effective and enable more organs to be transplanted. For example, the use of only parts of lungs and livers in transplants has made it easier to use live **donors** and has meant that more people can be helped by a single nonliving donor.

Drug companies are working toward new drugs to help with the problem of **rejection.** In particular, they are trying to develop drugs that will suppress the part of the **immune system** that causes the rejection of a transplanted organ yet will not suppress the body's natural defense against disease. The goal of all transplant research is to develop rejection-free transplants.

Although there are always new ideas, not all of them are successful. In the 1970s, Robert Jarvik designed an artificial heart that he hoped would provide a long-term function by removing the need for human donors and avoiding problems of rejection. A number of these artificial hearts were transplanted, and one patient, William Schroeder, lived for 620 days. However, the quality of life for these patients was not very good, and they suffered many **infections** and other problems. Eventually, doctors decided that the only real use for artificial hearts was to prolong a patient's life in the hope that a suitable donor might be found.

In 2001, surgeons and technicians made significant advances in the technology of artificial hearts. On July 2, a patient named Robert Tools became the first person to receive a new type of artificial heart. His operation took place at Jewish Hospital in Louisville, Kentucky. The heart was different than earlier artificial hearts in that it was designed to fit inside the body without any tubes or wires sticking out through the patient's skin. It was also different in that it was designed to be a permanent, working heart replacement. After living with the device for 151 days, Tools died from complications unrelated to his artificial heart. Other patients have received the heart and research continues.

How far can we go?

The idea of transplant surgery has grown and developed from a very experimental science in the last century to a well-accepted treatment for many different forms of organ failure. There are still problems that transplantation cannot overcome. If someone becomes severely brain-damaged in an accident, their organs can be used to give new life to others, but doctors cannot transplant a new brain and restore life within the damaged body of the victim.

However, there are many ways in which transplant medicine is a triumph of human endeavor. It can be used to help people of all ages. Tiny babies, children, teenagers, adults, and even relatively elderly people in their 70s have been given new **kidneys** and other organs that have restored their quality of life. Nothing can ease the loss of a loved one for donor families, but they can have the knowledge that their relatives have helped others to live. Taking a dying person and restoring them to health using the organs of another person seems almost unbelievable. Organ transplantation is a modern miracle of medicine.

When people have received a successful transplant, they can return to health and fitness. In many countries, transplant patients get together to compete in a whole range of different sports. In the British Transplant Games, all the competitors, up to 1,000 of them, have received a transplant of some sort.

Timeline

1902 The first successful **kidney** transplant (in a dog) is carried out by Emerich Ullman.

1940s Sir Peter Medawar and others begin to understand and explain the human **immune system.**

1954 The first successful human kidney transplant takes place in the United States between identical twin brothers. The transplanted kidney works for eight years.

1959 Doctors Joseph Murray and John Merrill carry out the first successful human kidney allograft between nonidentical twins.

1962 The first successful kidney transplant using a nonliving **donor** is carried out in the U.S. The kidney functions for 21 months.

1963 The first lung transplant is carried out by Dr. James Hardy in the U.S.

Bone marrow is transplanted for the first time, leading to revolution in the treatment of **cancers** such as leukemia.

1966 A successful pancreas transplant is carried out for the first time in the U.S.

1967 The first successful liver transplant is carried out by Dr. Thomas Starzl in the U.S. The liver functions for thirteen months.

The first successful human heart transplant is carried out by Dr. Christiaan Barnard in South Africa. The heart functions for eighteen days.

1969 The **fungus** *Beauveria nivea* is discovered. A chemical called **cyclosporine** could be isolated from the fungus.

1972 Jean Borel discovers the **immunosuppressant** properties of cyclosporine.

1980 Cyclosporine is first **synthesized.**

1981 The first successful heart-and-lung transplant takes place in the U.S. The new organs function for five years.

1982 The first artificial heart, the Jarvik 7, is transplanted into Barney Clarke.

1983 Cyclosporine is approved for use as an immunosuppressant drug.

1984 "Baby Faye" in the U.S. is given a baboon's heart that works for 20 days.

1987 The first **domino transplant** takes place.

Dr. Starzl is involved in the first successful transplant of several different **abdominal organs.**

1989 The first successful liver transplant from a living relative takes place in the U.S.

The first transplant of a complete small intestine.

1992 The first baboon to human liver transplant is carried out in the U.S. The **recipient** lives for 70 days.

First pig to human liver transplant. The recipient dies after two days.

1996 The first successful split-liver transplants take place, using the liver from a nonliving donor to give more than one recipient the chance of life.

1998 Human embryonic stem cells are **cultured** in the laboratory for the first time in the U.S.

2000 The second Jarvik artificial heart (Jarvik 2000) is first used. The patient lives for five months.

2001 Robert Tools lives for 151 days after receiving the first artificial heart replacement designed to be a permanent replacement for the human heart.

2002 Scientists at the University of Missouri and a company called PPL Therapeutics announced independently that they had cloned pigs whose organs would likely not be rejected by humans. The pigs lack the gene that produces a certain sugar that causes organ rejection.

Glossary

abdominal organs organs found in the center part of the body. For example, the digestive system and the kidneys.

ABO system method of classifying human blood in which a person may have type A, type B, type O, or type AB blood

AIDS (acquired immunodeficiency syndrome) condition caused by the HIV virus in which the immune system is severely weakened, leaving the patient vulnerable to other diseases, from which the patient eventually dies

air sacs tiny spaces in the lungs where gas exchange takes place

altruistic unselfish towards other people

antibodies special proteins made by the immune system that attach to any foreign antigens and inactivate the invading cell

antigens special marker molecules sticking out from the surface of cell membranes

arthritis inflammation of the joints, a condition that is often very painful and can be crippling

bone marrow soft tissue in the hollow sections of the bones where blood is made

cancer potentially fatal disease caused by the uncontrolled growth of cells

carbohydrates type of food molecule that acts as an energy source

carbon dioxide gas produced as a waste product of respiration by most living organisms

central nervous system linked system of nerves, including the brain and spinal cord, which carry electrical messages around the body

cholesterol type of fat that is present in most body tissues. It is thought to be involved in many forms of heart disease.

cirrhosis disease of the liver, often caused by excess alcohol intake, where the liver function is progressively lost due to fibrous tissues replacing normal liver cells

conception moment at which a sperm and an egg join together to create an embryo

culture to grow microorganisms or cells in the laboratory

cyclosporine drug that suppresses the reaction of the immune system to foreign cells

domino transplants transplants that provide organs for two recipients. A patient with diseased lungs but a healthy heart receives a heart-and-lung transplant, and their healthy heart is then donated to a patient needing a heart transplant.

donor someone who donates an organ (either when they are alive or after their death) to help someone who lacks this organ

embryo very early stages of human development in the uterus

ethical relating to what is morally right

fertilize to join a male and female sex cell together to form a new individual

fungus type of organism that produces spores, includes molds, yeast, and mushrooms

genetic diseases diseases that occur because of defects in the genes or chromosomes

genetic engineering process by which the genetic material of a cell may be altered either by replacing damaged genetic material or adding extra genetic material

graft to transplant a piece of tissue from one place on a person's body to another place, either on the same body or someone else's

heart attack when blood flow to the heart is reduced due to a blockage in the blood vessel, causing a sudden abnormality in the functioning of the heart

immune system system in the body that recognizes foreign cells and destroys them

immunosuppressant causing a reduction in the activity of the immune system

in vitro fertilization medical treatment in which an egg is fertilized outside of the body of the mother before being returned to her uterus

infection invasion of the body by microorganisms

kidney organ that removes waste urea and excess salt from the blood, producing urine that is passed into the bladder

lymphocytes white blood cells that make antibodies

membrane thin layer or "skin" around cells

microorganisms organisms, like bacteria, which are too small to see with the naked eye and need to be viewed through a microscope

molecule tiny particle, made up of two or more atoms joined together

organ systems collection of organs working together to carry out a major function in the body

placenta organ in the mother's uterus that supplies a developing baby with food and oxygen

protein type of food molecule important for building muscle and growth

recipient patient who receives a donated organ

rejection to refuse to accept; rejection of transplanted organs occurs when the body realizes they are not its own

scan way of looking into the body without opening it up. There are many different types of scan used by doctors in the diagnosis of disease and monitoring of health.

skin graft transplantation of healthy skin from one part of the body to another to cover and heal a large burn or wound

steroids lipid-based chemical. Some hormones are steroids and steroid drugs are used for a variety of reasons.

stroke sudden interruption of the brain's blood supply caused by the rupture of a blood vessel or a clot formation in the brain. These can damage the body's functioning and even cause death.

synthesize to make. Chemicals can be made artificially rather than extracted from a source such as a plant or animal.

tissue collection of cells in the body that all carry out the same function—for example, muscle tissue

toxin (toxic) poison (something that is poisonous)

urea toxic chemical made when excess protein is broken down in the body

uterus female organ in which the fetus develops

xenotransplantation transplanting an organ from one species of animal into another completely different species

Further Reading

Bankston, John. *Robert Jarvik and the First Artificial Heart.* Bear, Del.: Mitchell Lane Publishers, 2002.

Fullick, Ann. *The Human Body.* Chicago: Heinemann Library, 1999.

Kittredge, Mary. *Organ Transplants.* Broomall, Penn.: Chelsea House Publishers, 1999.

Snedden, Robert. *Fighting Infectious Diseases.* Chicago: Heinemann Library, 2000.

Index